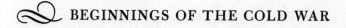 BEGINNINGS OF THE COLD WAR

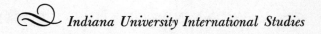
Indiana University International Studies

MARTIN F. HERZ

Beginnings
of the Cold War

INDIANA UNIVERSITY PRESS

BLOOMINGTON & LONDON

Contents

A Few Basic Texts

Passages from Allied declarations and agreements whose breach by the Soviet Union is discussed in this narrative.

ATLANTIC CHARTER, AUGUST 14, 1941

. . . First, their countries seek no aggrandizement, territorial or other;

Second, they desire to see no territorial changes that do not accord with the freely expressed wishes of the people concerned;

Third, they respect the right of all peoples to choose the form of government under which they will live; and they wish to see sovereign rights and self-government restored to those who have been forcibly deprived of them. . . .

Proclaimed by President Roosevelt and Prime Minister Churchill, subscribed to (with a reservation*) by the

* The Russian reservation was as follows:
"Considering that the practical application of these principles will necessarily adapt itself to the circumstances, needs, and historic

A Few Basic Texts

Soviet government on September 24, 1941; reaffirmed in the United Nations Declaration of January 1, 1942; reaffirmed in the Yalta Protocol of February 11, 1945

MOSCOW DECLARATION, NOVEMBER 1, 1943

. . . jointly declare:

6. That after the termination of hostilities they will not employ their military forces within the territories of other states except for the purposes envisaged in this declaration and after joint consultation.

> *Signed by Foreign Minister Molotov, Foreign Secretary Eden, Secretary of State Hull, and Chinese Ambassador Foo*

---

peculiarities of particular countries, the Soviet Government can state that a consistent application of these principles will secure the most energetic support on the part of the government and peoples of the Soviet Union." Statement by I. M. Maisky, Soviet ambassador to Great Britain, in accepting the principles of the Atlantic Charter on behalf of his government. *Report of Proceedings, Inter-Allied Meeting held in London at St. James Palace on September 24, 1941* (London: H. M. Stationery Office, 1941), Cmd. 6315. (This statement does not appear in the U.S. official documentation series published by the Department of State.) Cf. also Churchill's comment documented in note 11, chap. 2, below.

According to the Hull *Memoirs,* Maisky "indicated that his Government felt it should have been consulted beforehand regarding the Atlantic Charter." *The Memoirs of Cordell Hull* (New York: Macmillan, 1948), II, 1165. Proclamation of the Atlantic Charter took place two months after the German attack on Russia and one month after conclusion of the mutual assistance agreement between Great Britain and the Soviet Union.

As for Great Britain, Churchill declared that the Atlantic Charter would not apply to the British Empire. Speech to the House of Commons on September 9, 1941, *H. C. Debates, 5th series,* vol. 374, coll. 68-69.

A Few Basic Texts

... The establishment of order in Europe and the rebuilding of national economic life must be achieved by processes which will enable the liberated peoples to destroy the last vestiges of Nazism and Fascism and to create democratic institutions of their own choice. This is a principle of the Atlantic Charter—the right of all peoples to choose the form of government under which they will live—the restoration of sovereign rights and self-government to those peoples who have been forcibly deprived of them by the aggressor nations.

To foster the conditions in which the liberated peoples may exercise these rights, the three governments will jointly assist the people in any European liberated state or former Axis satellite state in Europe where in their judgment conditions require (a) to establish conditions of internal peace; (b) to carry out emergency measures for the relief of distressed peoples; (c) to form interim governmental authorities broadly representative of all democratic elements in the population and pledged to the earliest possible establishment through free elections of governments responsive to the will of the people; and (d) to facilitate where necessary the holding of such elections. . . .

When, in the opinion of the three governments, conditions in any European liberated state or any former Axis satellite state in Europe make such action necessary, they will immediately consult together on the measures necessary to discharge the joint responsibilities set forth in this declaration. . . .

Signed at Yalta by Prime Minister Churchill, President Roosevelt, and Premier Stalin.

DECLARATION ON POLAND, FEBRUARY 11, 1945

We came to the Crimea Conference resolved to settle our differences about Poland. . . . We reaffirm our common desire to see established a strong, free, independent and democratic Poland. As a result of our discussions, we have agreed on the conditions in which a new Polish Provisional Government of National Unity may be formed in such a manner as to command recognition by the three major powers. . . .

A new situation has been created in Poland as a result of her complete liberation by the Red Army. This calls for the establishment of a Polish Provisional Government which can be more broadly based than was possible before the recent liberation of western Poland. The Provisional Government which is now functioning in Poland should therefore be reorganized on a broader democratic basis with the inclusion of democratic leaders from Poland itself and from Poles abroad. This new Government should then be called the Polish Provisional Government of National Unity.

. . . This Polish Provisional Government of National Unity shall be pledged to the holding of free and unfettered elections as soon as possible on the basis of universal suffrage and secret ballot. In these elections all democratic and anti-Nazi parties shall have the right to take part and to put forward candidates. . . .

> *Signed at Yalta by Prime Minister Churchill, President Roosevelt, and Marshal Stalin*

 BEGINNINGS OF THE COLD WAR

1

Introduction and Perspective

I call this little book an analytical compilation. It is a modest effort with a limited purpose. It does not try to lay bare the ideological roots of the Cold War, which other authors have done very well, or to survey its entire development. The purpose of this study is, simply, to summarize and highlight a few chapters of recent world history which encompass the major *beginnings* of the Cold War.

When did the Cold War begin? Its origins go back, no doubt, to Marx and Lenin. Experts may differ as to when, after the last war, the term "Cold War" became applicable to our relations with Soviet Russia. But surely the period covered here—essentially, the early months of 1945—helps to understand how it came about that we and the Russians weren't able to exist together more peacefully after World War II.

This summary represents something I had wanted to do for many years. Human memory being limited, it is perhaps not surprising that so many of us in the Foreign Service who lived through that period have forgotten just how our present conflict with Soviet Russia came to pass. Of course, we all know most of the important elements, but we have forgotten the sequence of events, and even some important facts have sunk below the level of ready recall.

We need to remember.

Also, it occurred to me that if the memories of those of us who lived through that period are no longer fresh, how much more difficult it must be for our younger colleagues in the Foreign Service, who were still in school at that time and who probably didn't follow the events even in the newspapers, to put the basic facts into perspective. They may not have found it possible to consult the many official documents and biographies and other works of scholarship on the subject.

For the existing source material is overwhelming. Virtually everything of significance has long since been published. The trouble is that the subject matter is complicated, and it takes a great deal of time to sift through even the most important material. If the Department of State had not assigned me to the Senior Seminar in Foreign Policy, thus giving me time for reading, study and reflection, I should not have been able to undertake this task.

And this is a suitable point at which to state that although in surveying the available historical material I received help from many quarters, including some friends in the Department of State, any views expressed in this book are those of the author and do not necessarily represent the views of the United States government. As will be seen, however, the author expresses few views of his own in this book. Essentially, we are surveying historical facts—but of course the highlighting of those facts and the significance attributed to them are always matters of individual judgment.

One of the things that strikes one most forcefully as one starts out on such a retrospective enterprise is that our memories are selective and that, especially, we tend to forget our *expectations*. This is a strange psychological phenomenon. When an important event comes to pass, our recollection of the actual event is likely to overlay, to supersede, to crowd out the memory of our original expectations about that event.

Let me cite some examples which have a bearing on this study:

We all know that Japan capitulated about three months after the end of the war in Europe, but how many of us remember our earlier expectations about the duration of the Pacific war? We read today with amazement that at the Yalta Conference the Combined (U. S.-British) Chiefs of Staff recommended that "the planning date for the end of the war against Japan should be set at eighteen months after the defeat of Germany."[1] Today, of course, we have the benefit of hindsight. We know that the atomic bomb became available, and we know that even without the atomic bomb Japan would probably have been forced to give up, alone through bombing and the attrition on her shipping, perhaps not very long after we had captured Okinawa and Iwo Jima in the spring of 1945. That, however, was emphatically not the view of our most qualified military men in the early months of that year.

In the judgment of our most qualified military leaders, the entry of Russia into the war against Japan was highly desirable. We note, in particular, that our Joint Staff planners considered it militarily important that Russia "conduct an all-out offensive against Manchuria to contain Japanese forces and resources in North China and Manchuria that might otherwise be employed in the defense of Japan."[2] Ten years later, one of our most illustrious military leaders publicly denied that he had favored Russia's entry into the war against Japan.[3] He was a victim of the phenomenon that I describe. His earlier anticipations were obviously overlaid, superseded, crowded out by his knowledge that, as it turned out, we did not need Russian help. The Department of Defense, after some historical research, brought out documentary evidence that the illustrious military leader had himself clearly advocated Russia's entry into the war even as a specific preparation for the launching of our own invasion of the Japanese home islands.[4] So fallible is human memory, especially when it comes to expectations.

Or take our expectations about the postwar period. How many of us remember our enormous preoccupation, as the war drew to its end, with the problems of "reconversion" and unemployment when, as it seemed, our vastly increased industrial potential would be no longer fully needed? Those who, like myself, had been unemployed before the war remember this poignantly, but even then we are in retrospect astounded by the statistics about U.S. unemployment immediately prior to our entry into the war: it had been 10.4 million in 1938, 9.4 million in 1939, and still 8.1 million in 1940 when the impact of the European war began to be felt. (By comparison, unemployment during the height of the depression had been 12.8 million,[5] in 1933.) We had been in what was termed an economic "recession" before World War II and there was widespread fear that the aftermath would involve another such prolonged period of under-use of our economy.

Is it surprising, then, to recall—even if it requires quite an effort—that the rush of our army to demobilize, the whole sentiment in favor of the speediest possible return of our soldiers, was not unrelated to the quest for jobs? We all wanted to get home quickly because those who would return last were expected to have the hardest times ahead of them. Today we know that no postwar recession developed and that, in fact, we soon moved into a period of further economic expansion. But most of our economic experts, and certainly the general public in the United States, had no such expectations in early 1945.

Nor, one may assume, did the Russians—steeped in the teachings of Marx and Lenin—have any expectation that the United States would be able to use its productive plant to capacity after the war. They were, as a matter of fact, reinforced in their expectations by the fact that the United States seemed interested in long-term credit arrangements for postwar trade with Russia. Thus Donald Nelson, chairman of the War Production Board, talked with Stalin and Mikoyan as early as October 1943 about the expected great American postwar "surplus" that would be available on advantageous terms to our Russian partners;[6] and in July 1944 Eric Johnston, president of the U.S. Chamber of Commerce, discussed the possibility of large-scale American postwar credits with the same Russian leaders.[7] How this expectation was disappointed will be part of our narrative.

The most important expectation, of course, related to the political shape of the postwar world. Here again, our knowledge of what actually happened may dim our recollection of the great hopes most of us held for a future of peace, order, and democratic development throughout the length and breadth of the world. For this purpose, the complete defeat and "re-education" of the Axis aggressors was our first requirement. The second requirement, it seemed, was a new world organization in which disputes would henceforth be settled on their merits. It seemed inconceivable that the world would break up into separate camps or spheres of influence, and the full weight of American diplomacy was directed to the avoidance of a political line of demarcation across Europe.

We were, or so it seemed, summoned once more by history to take a leading role in the establishment of a world organization to keep the peace, in partnership with our wartime allies. However, we were not ready for a world parliament in which constraints might be applied against us. "The veto power," Cordell Hull told a group of Congressional leaders in 1944, "is in the document [of proposals for the future United Nations organization] primarily on account of the United States. It is a necessary safeguard in dealing with a new and untried world arrangement. . . . We cannot move any faster than an alert public opinion in perfecting a permanent peace organization, but we should not be deterred for an instant from pursuing the sole course that is open, the alternative being international chaos such as we have had heretofore."[8]

While great hopes were placed in the future world organization (which had no name as yet, for the words "United Nations" originally applied only to the wartime alliance), there were doubts whether Russia would cooperate with it wholeheartedly. Accordingly, there was rejoicing when the Yalta Conference seemed to have brought agreement on the voting arrangements for the new organization; and there was dismay when Russia announced in March 1945 that it would not send Foreign Minister Molotov to the San Francisco Conference, where the new organization was to be formally created. How many of our hopes rode on the future world organization is apparent from rereading the newspapers of those days. Indeed, our disappointments over the abuse of the veto in the United Nations were a measure of our erstwhile expectation that, somehow, that organization would abate all frictions and rivalries between the great powers.

Yes, we were comrades-in-arms with Russia and we looked forward to a long period of peace and ever increasing cooperation and understanding. There were difficulties and troubles that came to the fore increasingly as the year 1945 wore on. They will be described and summarized. But there were also many things the general public did not know. We did not know, for instance, that Stalin in March 1945 had accused Churchill and Roosevelt in highly offensive terms of negotiating with Germany behind his back. We did not know of the acrimonious correspondence between these leaders about fulfillment of the Yalta Agreement on Poland. Throughout the war, information damaging to the alliance was purposely withheld from the American public, and some was withheld even after the defeat of Germany.

An American officer, for instance, who returned from a prisoner-of-war camp in Germany and presented evidence to our War Department that the Russians had been guilty of massacring thousands of Polish officers at Katyn (as had been claimed by Nazi propaganda during the war) received a letter ordering him "neither to mention nor discuss this matter with anyone in or out of the service without specific approval in writing from the War Department." Many years later, in 1952, the general who had issued that order was summoned before a committee of our House of Representatives and gave an explanation which thoroughly reflects our attitudes and expectations in early 1945.

Said Major General Clayton Bissell with soldierly directness: "I was very concerned all of this particular time with events that were even more critical to America's war with Japan, and this [disclosure] wasn't going to help win the Japanese war one bit, except in a different way. And that was the reason I was so careful about this thing. . . . Our number one objective, other than defeating Japan at that time, was to get the UNO going. We didn't know whether we could get Russia to come in."[9]

9

The Katyn massacre, as we shall see, played a fateful role in the political history of the war and of the postwar settlements.

How well I personally recall the attitude reflected in General Bissell's statement! I was among the first American officers to enter Vienna in the summer of 1945, after the Russians had been in occupation there for four months, raping and pillaging on an enormous scale. Hardly had we arrived when we were inundated with stories about the misdeeds of the Russian soldiery. We turned those stories aside with remarks that the Russians were our allies; that they had suffered terribly in the war; that we intended to fight jointly with them to bring about the defeat of Japan; and that we hoped to cooperate with them, however difficult it might be, to assure the peace of the world. This was a widespread attitude, for an enormous amount of good will for Russia had accumulated in the United States during the war.[10] How this good will was quickly dissipated in the space of very few months is the subject of this narrative.

There can be no better way to start our consideration of the evidence than to examine one of the most fascinating diplomatic documents of the period, the record of the conversations between Harry L. Hopkins and Josef Stalin in which they reviewed the reasons—some apparent, some real—why relations between the wartime allies were so rapidly deteriorating. The time of the first conversation was May 26, 1945, three weeks after the defeat of Germany. The place was Stalin's office in the Kremlin. Present were, on the Russian side, Marshal Stalin, Foreign Minister Vyacheslav Molotov, and Mr. Pavlov, an interpreter; and on the American side, Mr. Hopkins, Ambassador W. Averell Harriman, and Mr. Charles E. Bohlen. There were six conversations between these men in the space of ten days, reviewing some of the root causes of the Cold War.

Introduction and Perspective

Hopkins had only a few more months to live. He had risen from a hospital bed to be present at the funeral service for President Roosevelt, whom he had served in many capacities including that of Secretary of Commerce and, more important, as personal assistant, agent, and confidant. For almost four years he had lived in the White House. He had been present at the Tehran and Yalta Conferences, though at the latter he had been too ill to attend all the meetings. He had been bedridden in his home when President Truman asked him to undertake this mission to Moscow. The new President felt that Hopkins was best able to interpret the American position to Stalin because he had been so closely associated with President Roosevelt and because of the role he had played in starting the program of American aid that had meant so much to Russia during the war.

The careful reader will note in the next following narrative chapter the differing meanings attached by Hopkins and Stalin to the phrases "friendly government" and "strong and democratic Poland"; the use of the words "vital interest" by Stalin to describe the Russian desire for what he called a "strong and friendly Poland"; and the growing bluntness of Hopkins in describing Poland as the test case of American-Russian postwar relations. Although the United States had many other grievances against the Soviet Union stemming from unilateral actions in eastern Europe—some of which will be brought out in later sections of this study—the Hopkins conversations revolved very largely around the Polish question.

Russia lost about 15,000,000 dead in World War II, or 9 per cent of its population. The United States lost about 400,000 dead, or 0.3 per cent of its population. But the country that lost the greatest proportion, 14 per cent of its population, was Poland. Out of a prewar population of 35,000,000, it lost approximately 5,000,000 dead.[11] This becomes understandable when we think about the unique position of Poland as the only country that was attacked by *both* Germany and the Soviet Union during the same war and that experienced the full fury of both totalitarian occupations and of mass exterminations, plus a civil war between two rival undergrounds. It is useful to keep this background in mind as one reads the following narrative.

At the time that we are discussing here, the term "satellite" was not yet used to describe states subservient to and controlled by the Soviet Union. (The term was then used to describe Rumania, Bulgaria and Hungary, which were, or had been, in the sphere of influence of Nazi Germany.) It is well to recall, at the same time, that the Western hemisphere was regarded not only by us but also by our allies as an absolute preserve of the United States. The idea that Cuba, for instance, or any other neighbor of the United States might adopt a system or an allegiance hostile to the United States would at that time have seemed utterly fantastic. As far as Europe was concerned, the United States would not hear of spheres of influence and, as we shall see, throughout the period reviewed in this study we felt that Russian security could be adequately protected by freely elected governments in the countries on Russia's borders. But it soon turned out that such governments would—for good reason—have been bitterly hostile to the Soviet Union; and, as we shall see at the end of Chapter 5, that damaging fact was even admitted by Stalin at the Potsdam Conference.

Poland was the most important case in point, as is clearly brought out in the Stalin-Hopkins conversations summarized in the next chapter.

NOTES

1. Report of the Combined Chiefs of Staff to President Roosevelt and Prime Minister Churchill, 9 February 1945, in *Foreign Relations of the United States—The Conferences of Malta and Yalta* (Washington: Government Printing Office, 1955, hereafter cited as *Yalta Papers*), p. 830.

2. Report by the Joint Staff Planners, 18 January 1945, Conclusions, para. 6 b. (1) (a) (ii). Ibid., p. 392.

The Joint Chiefs of Staff, in a memorandum to the President dated January 23, 1945, stated that "Russia's entry at as early a date as possible consistent with her ability to engage in offensive operations is necessary to provide maximum assistance to our Pacific operations." Ibid., p. 396.

3. General Douglas MacArthur declared on March 23, 1955 that his views had not been sought for the Yalta Conference, but that if they had he "would most emphatically have recommended against bringing the Soviet into the Pacific war at that late date." *New York Times*, March 24, 1955.

4. U. S. Department of Defense, *The Entry of the Soviet Union into the War Against Japan: Military Plans, 1941-1945*—press release of October 19, 1955, in *New York Times* of October 20, 1955. Report by Brig. Gen. George A. Lincoln of his conversation with Gen. MacArthur on February 25, 1945: "Concerning over-all plan, General MacArthur considers it essential that maximum number of Jap divisions be engaged and pinned down on Asiatic mainland before United States forces strike Japan proper." Also memorandum by Col. Paul L. Freeman, Jr. on conversation with Gen. MacArthur on February 13, 1945: "He [Gen. MacArthur] was in thorough agreement that the only means of defeating Japan was by the invasion of the industrial heart of Japan. He stressed the potency of the Japanese Army and stated that when we entered Japan we must be prepared to reckon with the Japanese Army in far greater strength than is now there. He was apprehensive as to the possibility of the movement of the bulk of the Manchurian Army and other Japanese forces from China to the defense of the homeland. He emphatically stated that

13

we must not invade Japan proper unless the Russian Army is previously committed to action in Manchuria. . . ."

Cf. also *The Forrestal Diaries* (New York: Viking, 1951), p. 31, entry for Wednesday, February 28, 1945: "On the . . . question of the war against Japan afterward, he [MacArthur] expressed the view that the help of the Chinese would be negligible. He felt that we should secure the commitment of the Russians to active and vigorous prosecution of a campaign against the Japanese in Manchukuo of such proportions as to pin down a very large part of the Japanese Army; that once this campaign was engaged, we should then launch an attack on the home islands, giving, as he expressed it, the *coup de main* from the rear while substantial portions of the military power of Japan were engaged on the mainland of Asia. . . . He said he felt that our strength should be reserved for use in the Japanese mainland, on the plain of Tokyo, and that this could not be done without the assurance that the Japanese would be heavily engaged by the Russians in Manchuria. He expressed doubt that the use of anything less than sixty divisions by Russia would be sufficient. . . ."

5. U.S. Department of Commerce, *Historical Statistics of the United States* (Washington: Government Printing Office, 1957), p. 73.

6. Herbert Feis, *Churchill, Roosevelt, Stalin—The War They Waged and the Peace They Sought* (Princeton, N.J.: Princeton University Press, 1957), p. 641.

7. *New York Times,* July 14, 1944.

8. *The Memoirs of Cordell Hull* (New York: Macmillan, 1948), II, 1662. Mr. Hull added, however, that it was his expectation that "none of the permanent members of the Council would exercise its right of veto capriciously or arbitrarily" and that any of the great powers would "call this [veto] power forth only on a matter of the gravest concern to itself, never on secondary matters and never in a way to prevent thorough discussion of any issue" (II, 1663).

9. *Hearings Before the Select Committee to Conduct an Investigation of the Facts, Evidence and Circumstances of the Katyn Forest Massacre,* 82nd Congress, House, Second Session, February/March 1952 (hereafter cited as *Katyn Forest Massacre*), p. 1877.

10. Secretary of State James F. Byrnes, for instance, reconstructed this state of mind as follows in 1947: "It is a trite but true statement that 'hindsight is better than foresight'. But, if one can recall the

attitude of the people of the United States toward the Soviets in the days immediately following the German surrender, he will agree that, as a result of our sufferings and sacrifices in a common cause, the Soviet Union then had in the United States a deposit of good will, as great, if not greater, than that of any other country. It is little short of a tragedy that Russia should have withdrawn that deposit with the recklessness and the lack of appreciation shown during the last two and a half years. Our assumption that we could co-operate, and our patience in trying to co-operate, justify the firmness we now must show." *Speaking Frankly* (New York: Harper, 1947), p. 71.

11. Encyclopaedia Britannica, Inc., *10 Eventful Years* (Chicago, 1947). Population figures for Russia from the 1939 census; for the United States, from the 1940 census; and for Poland, estimated as of 1939. Casualty figures for Russia have never been published and are unofficial estimates. The U.S. casualty figure is based on official sources. Polish casualties are estimated and include some 3,000,000 Jews murdered in Nazi concentration camps.

According to some Polish sources, Poland lost not 5 but 6 million human.lives during the war. Cf. Stanislaw Mikolajczyk, *The Rape of Poland—Pattern of Soviet Aggression* (New York: McGraw-Hill, 1948), p. 123.

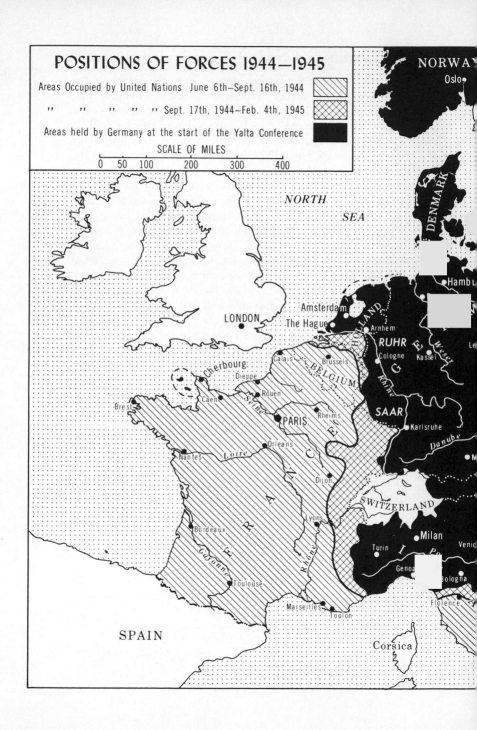

POSITIONS OF FORCES 1944—1945

Areas Occupied by United Nations June 6th—Sept. 16th, 1944

 ,,   ,,   ,,   ,,   ,, Sept. 17th, 1944—Feb. 4th, 1945

Areas held by Germany at the start of the Yalta Conference

SCALE OF MILES

0   50   100   200   300   400

NORWAY

Oslo

DENMARK

Hambu

NORTH

SEA

Amsterdam

The Hague

HOLLAND

Arnhem

RUHR

Cologne   Kassel   Le

Weser

LONDON

Calais

Dieppe

BELGIUM

Brussels

Cherbourg

Rouen

Rhine

Caen

Seine

SAAR

Karlsruhe

Brest

Rheims

PARIS

Danube

Nantes

Loire

Orleans

Dijon

SWITZERLAND

FRANCE

Bordeaux

Lyons

Milan

Turin   I   Venic

Garonne

Rhône

Genoa   Bologna

Toulouse

Marseilles

Florence

Toulon

SPAIN

Corsica

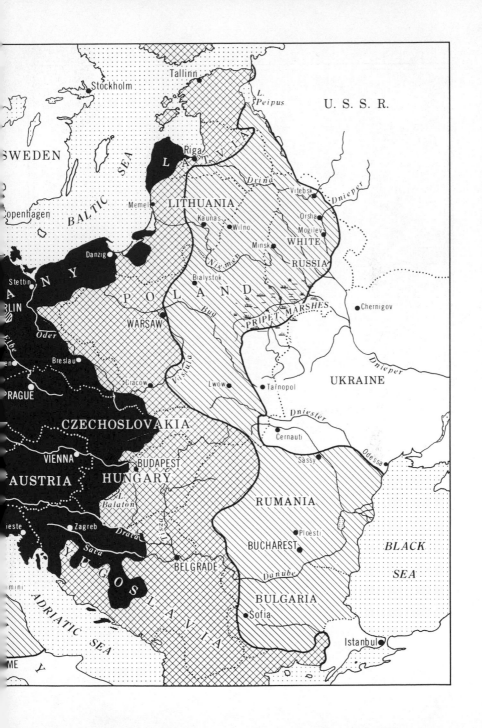

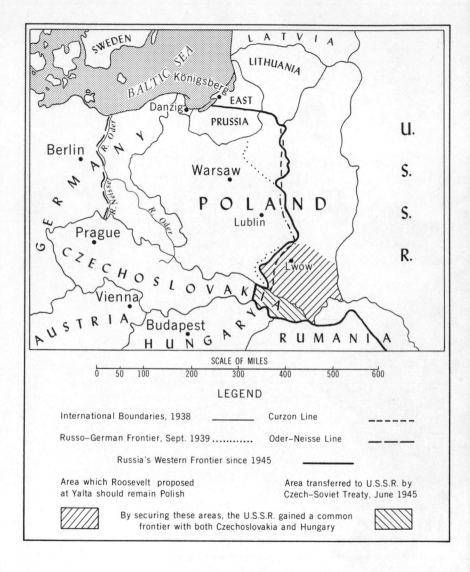

SCALE OF MILES

| 0 | 50 | 100 | 200 | 300 | 400 | 500 | 600 |

LEGEND

International Boundaries, 1938   _____   Curzon Line   — — — — —

Russo–German Frontier, Sept. 1939 ....   Oder–Neisse Line   — — — —

Russia's Western Frontier since 1945   _____

Area which Roosevelt proposed
at Yalta should remain Polish

Area transferred to U.S.S.R. by
Czech–Soviet Treaty, June 1945

By securing these areas, the U.S.S.R. gained a common
frontier with both Czechoslovakia and Hungary

2

Stalin-Hopkins Conversations

EXTRACT FROM THE BOHLEN MINUTES[1]

Mr. Hopkins began the conversation by reporting on the circumstances of the death of President Roosevelt six weeks before. He said that on his trip home from Yalta the President had frequently reviewed with him the results of the Crimea Conference and that he had come away from the Conference with renewed confidence that the United States and the Soviet Union could work together in peace as they had in war. President Roosevelt on the trip home had frequently spoken of the respect and admiration he had for Marshal Stalin and he had looked forward to their next meeting which the President hoped would be in Berlin.

Marshal Stalin remarked that he recalled the toast at the Crimea Conference to their next meeting in Berlin.

Mr. Hopkins said that he recalled his first meeting with the Marshal in July 1941, during the troubled and anxious days of the German offensive. He said he remembered vividly the

19

frankness with which Marshal Stalin had told him of the Soviet position and of the unalterable determination of the Soviet Union to wage war against Germany until final victory was assured. He had returned to the United States and conveyed to President Roosevelt his own conviction that the Soviet Union would hold fast and President Roosevelt had thereupon initiated the program of assistance to the Soviet Union. At that time, most people believed that a German victory was inevitable but President Roosevelt, in spite of all such opinions, had decided otherwise and through his leadership he had put through a program of aid to Russia.

Marshal Stalin observed that at that time there had been many doubts of the ability of the Soviet Union to keep going. . . .

Mr. Hopkins then said that a few days ago President Truman had sent for him and had asked him to come to Moscow to have a talk with Marshal Stalin. There were a number of things that he and Mr. Harriman hoped to discuss with Marshal Stalin and Mr. Molotov while he was in Moscow, but before going into those specific questions he wished to tell the Marshal of the real reason why the President had asked him to come, and that was the question of the fundamental relationship between the U. S. and the Soviet Union.

Two months ago, Mr. Hopkins said, there had been overwhelming sympathy among the American people for the Soviet Union and complete support for President Roosevelt's policies which the Marshal knew so well. . . . The American people at that time hoped and confidently believed that the two countries could work together in peace as well as they had in war. Mr. Hopkins said there had always been a small minority, the Hearsts and the McCormicks, who had been against the policy of cooperation with the Soviet Union. These men had also been bitter political enemies of President Roosevelt but had never had any backing from the American people as was shown by the fact that against their bitter opposition President Roosevelt had been four times elected President. He said he did not intend to discuss this small minority but to discuss the general state of American opinion and particularly the present attitude of the millions of Americans who had supported President Roosevelt's policy in regard to the Soviet Union and who believed that despite the different political and economic ideologies of the two countries, the U. S. and the Soviet Union could work together after the war in order to bring about a secure peace for humanity.

Mr. Hopkins said he wished to assure the Marshal with all the earnestness at his command that this body of American public opinion who had been the constant support of the Roosevelt policies were seriously disturbed about our relations with Russia. In fact, in the last six weeks the deterioration of public opinion had been so serious as to affect adversely the relations between our two countries. He said he wished to emphasize that this change had occurred in the very people who had supported to the hilt Roosevelt's policy of cooperation with the Soviet Union. . . . It was obvious to them that if present trends continued unchecked the entire structure of world cooperation and relations with the Soviet Union which President Roosevelt and the Marshal had labored so hard to build would be destroyed.

Prior to his departure, Mr. Hopkins continued, President Truman had expressed to him his great anxiety at the present situation and also his desire to continue President Roosevelt's policy of working with the Soviet Union and his intention to carry out in fact as well as in spirit all the arrangements, both formal and informal, which President Roosevelt and Marshal Stalin had worked out together. Mr. Hopkins added that as

21

the Marshal knew he had not been well and he would not be in Moscow unless he had felt the situation was serious. He also said he would not have come had he not believed that the present trend could be halted and a common basis found to go forward in the future.

Mr. Hopkins said that it was not simple or easy to put a finger on the precise reasons for this deterioration but he must emphasize that without the support of public opinion and particularly of the supporters of President Roosevelt it would be very difficult for President Truman to carry forward President Roosevelt's policy. He said that, as the Marshal was aware, the cardinal basis of President Roosevelt's policy which the American people had fully supported had been the concept that the interests of the U. S. were world-wide and not confined to North and South America and the Pacific Ocean and it was this concept that had led to the many conferences concerning the peace of the world which President Roosevelt had had with Marshal Stalin. President Roosevelt had believed that the Soviet Union had likewise world-wide interests and that the two countries could work out together any political or economic considerations at issue between them.

After the Yalta Conference, Mr. Hopkins continued, it looked as though we were well on the way to reaching a basic understanding on all questions of foreign affairs of interest to our respective countries. . . . He said in a country like ours public opinion is affected by specific incidents and in this case the deterioration in public opinion in regard to our relations with the Soviet Union had been centered in our inability to carry into effect the Yalta Agreement on Poland. There were also a train of events, each unimportant in themselves, which had grown up around the Polish question and which contributed to the deterioration in public opinion. President Truman felt, and so did the

American public, although they were not familiar with all the details, a sense of bewilderment at our inability to solve the Polish question.

Marshal Stalin replied that the reason for the failure on the Polish question was that the Soviet Union desired to have a friendly Poland, but that Great Britain wanted to revive the system of *cordon sanitaire** on the Soviet borders.

Mr. Hopkins replied that neither the Government nor the people of the U. S. had any such intention. . . . He stated that the U. S. would desire a Poland friendly to the Soviet Union and in fact desired to see friendly countries all along the Soviet borders.

Marshal Stalin replied if that be so we could easily come to terms in regard to Poland.

Mr. Hopkins said that during his visit there were a number of specific questions that he and Mr. Harriman hoped to discuss with Marshal Stalin and Mr. Molotov but that the general statement he had just made concerning public opinion in the U. S. was the principal reason for his coming and the principal cause of anxiety at the present time. He said he had wished to state frankly and as forcibly as he knew how to Marshal Stalin the importance that he, personally, attached to the present trend of events and that he felt that the situation would get rapidly worse unless we could clear up the Polish matter. He had therefore been glad to hear the Marshal say that he thought the question could be settled.

[Hopkins then detailed the matters he hoped to discuss during his stay in Moscow, reemphasizing the importance of the Polish question, and Stalin said that he had also several disturbing questions on his mind in regard to the United States. It

* The post-World-War-I system of anti-Communist buffer states on Russia's borders in Europe.

was agreed to pursue these matters at a later meeting. These were subsequently discussed the evening of May 27, as follows, still according to the Bohlen minutes:]

Marshal Stalin said he would not attempt to use Soviet public opinion as a screen but would speak of the feeling that had been created in Soviet governmental circles as a result of recent moves on the part of the U. S. Government. He said these circles felt a certain alarm in regard to the attitude of the U. S. Government. It was their impression that the American attitude towards the Soviet Union had perceptibly cooled once it became obvious that Germany was defeated, and that it was as though the Americans were saying that the Russians were no longer needed. He said he would give the following examples:

(1) The case of Argentina and its invitation to the San Francisco Conference. At Yalta, it had been agreed that only those states which had declared war on Germany before the first of March would be invited, but at San Francisco this decision had been overturned. He said it was not understood in the Soviet Union why Argentina could not have been asked to wait three months or so before joining the world organization. He added that the action of the Conference and the attitude of the U. S. had raised the question of the value of agreements between the three major powers if their decisions could be overturned by the votes of such countries as Honduras and Porto Rico [sic].

(2) The question of the Reparations Commission. At Yalta, it had been agreed that the three powers would sit on this Commission in Moscow and subsequently the U. S. had insisted that France should be represented on the same basis as the Soviet Union. This he felt was an insult to the Soviet Union in view of the fact that France had concluded a separate peace with Germany and had opened the frontier to the Germans. . . . To at-

tempt to place France on the same footing as the Soviet Union looked like an attempt to humiliate the Russians.

(3) The attitude of the U. S. Government towards the Polish question. He said that at Yalta it had been agreed that the existing government was to be reconstructed and that anyone with common sense could see that this meant that the present government was to form the basis of the new. He said no other understanding of the Yalta Agreement was possible. Despite the fact that they were simple people the Russians should not be regarded as fools, which was a mistake the West frequently made, nor were they blind and could quite well see what was going on before their eyes. It was true that the Russians were patient in the interests of a common cause but their patience had its limits.

(4) The manner in which Lend-Lease had been curtailed. If the U. S. was unable to supply the Soviet Union further under Lend-Lease that was one thing but that the manner in which it had been done had been unfortunate and even brutal. For example, certain ships had been unloaded and while it was true that this order had been cancelled the whole manner in which it had been done had caused concern to the Soviet Government. If the refusal to continue Lend-Lease was designed as pressure on the Russians in order to soften them up then it was a fundamental mistake. Marshal Stalin said he must tell Mr. Hopkins frankly that if the Russians were approached frankly on a friendly basis much could be done but that reprisals in any form would bring about the exact opposite effect.

(5) The disposition of the German Navy and merchant fleet which surrendered to the Allies. Stalin said that as we knew certain units of the German Army who had been fighting against the Russians had been anxious to surrender to the Western allies but not to the Russians, but under the surrender terms

German troops were supposed to surrender to the army against which they had fought. He said, for example, General Eisenhower as an honest man had correctly turned over to the Soviet Command in Czechoslovakia some 135,000 German troops who had tried to surrender to the American Army. This was an example of fair and honest behavior. However, as regards the German fleet which had caused so much damage to Leningrad and other Soviet ports not one vessel had been turned over to the Soviet Union. . . . He said that the Soviet Government had certain information leading it to believe that both the U. S. and England intended to reject the Soviet request and he must say that if this turned out to be true it would be very unpleasant. The Marshal concluded by saying that he had completed the range of his account.

Mr. Hopkins said he first of all wished to express appreciation of the frankness with which Marshal Stalin had exposed his worries. [He then proceeded to explain the U. S. position on the German naval vessels, which was that we did not intend to keep any of them, and then went into a lengthy explanation of the status of Lend-Lease during and after the European war, concluding that the incident to which Marshal Stalin referred did not have any fundamental policy significance.]

Marshal Stalin said he wished to make it clear that he fully understood the right of the U. S. to curtail Lend-Lease shipments to the Soviet Union under present conditions . . . but what he had in mind was the manner and form in which it was done. He felt that what was after all an agreement between the two Governments had been ended in a scornful and abrupt manner. . . . He added that the Soviet Government had intended to make a suitable expression of gratitude to the U. S. for the Lend-Lease assistance during the war but the way in which this program had been halted now made that impossible.

Mr. Hopkins replied that what disturbed him most about the Marshal's statement was the revelation that he believed that the U. S. would use Lend-Lease as a means of showing our displeasure with the Soviet Union. He wished to assure the Marshal that however unfortunate the impression this question had caused in the mind of the Soviet Government, he must believe that there was no attempt or desire on the part of the U. S. to use it as a pressure weapon. He said the U. S. is a strong power and does not go in for those methods. Furthermore, we have no conflict of immediate interests with the Soviet Union and would have no reason to adopt such practices.

[Hopkins then turned to the question of the Reparations Commission. He pointed out, *inter alia*, that in any event the three powers would in the first instance begin their discussions in Moscow without France. Marshal Stalin replied that Poland, which had suffered even more than France, should certainly be represented if France was to be, and that Yugoslavia also deserved a place. The discussion then turned to the Argentine question. Ambassador Harriman explained that the U. S. had obtained Latin American support for the admission of the Ukraine and White Russia as separate members of the new world organization, as had been agreed at Yalta. However, the Latin American countries had immediately tried to connect this question with that of the admission of the Argentine. Mr. Stettinius had made it plain that he would not make any such connection and in the end the Latin American countries did vote solidly in support of the Yalta decision regarding Ukraine and White Russia. Mr. Harriman said that if Mr. Molotov had not then introduced the question of an invitation to the Warsaw Government, we might have been successful in persuading the Latin American countries to postpone the question of Argentina. Marshal Stalin finally said that in any event what had been done

27

could not be put right and the Argentine question now belonged to the past.]

Mr. Hopkins then said with the Marshal's permission he would like to review the position of the U. S. in regard to Poland. He said first of all he wished to assure the Marshal that he had no thought or indeed any right to attempt to settle the Polish problem during his visit here in Moscow, nor was he intending to hide behind American public opinion in presenting the position of the U. S.

Marshal Stalin said he was afraid that his remark concerning Soviet public opinion had cut Mr. Hopkins to the quick and that he had not meant to imply that Mr. Hopkins was hiding behind the screen of American public opinion. In fact, he knew Mr. Hopkins to be an honest and frank man.

Mr. Hopkins said that he wished to state this position as clearly and as forcibly as he knew how. He said the question of Poland *per se* was not so important as the fact that it had become a symbol of our ability to work out problems with the Soviet Union. He said that we had no special interests in Poland and no special desire to see any particular kind of government, that we would accept any government in Poland which was desired by the Polish people and was at the same time friendly to the Soviet Government. He said that the people and Government of the U. S. felt that this was a problem which should be worked out jointly between the U. S., the Soviet Union and Great Britain and that we felt that the Polish people should be given the right to free elections to choose their own government and their own system and that Poland should genuinely be independent.

The Government and people of the U. S., Mr. Hopkins continued, were disturbed because the preliminary steps towards

28

the reestablishment of Poland appeared to have been taken unilaterally by the Soviet Union together with the present Warsaw Government and that in fact the U. S. was completely excluded. He said he hoped that Stalin would believe him when he said that this feeling was a fact. . . . He hoped that the Marshal would put his mind to the task of thinking up what diplomatic methods could be used to settle this question, keeping in mind the feeling of the American people. . . . Poland had become a symbol in the sense that it bore a direct relation to the willingness of the U. S. to participate in international affairs on a world-wide basis and that our people must believe that they are joining their power with that of the Soviet Union and Great Britain in the promotion of international peace and the well-being of humanity.

Mr. Hopkins concluded by saying that he felt the overwhelming majority of the people of the U. S. felt that the relations between the U.S. and the USSR could be worked out in a spirit of cooperation despite the differences in ideology and that with all these factors in its favor he wished to appeal to the Marshal to help find a way to the solution of the Polish problem.

Marshal Stalin replied that he wished Mr. Hopkins would take into consideration the following factors: He said it may seem strange, although it appeared to be recognized in U. S. circles and Churchill in his speeches also recognized it, that the Soviet Government should wish for a friendly Poland. In the course of twenty-five years the Germans had twice invaded Russia via Poland. Neither the British nor American people had experienced such German invasions which were a horrible thing to endure and the results of which were not easily forgotten. He said these German invasions were not warfare but were like the incursions of the Huns. He said that Germany had been able to do this because Poland had been regarded as a part of the *cordon sanitaire* around the Soviet Union and that previous European policy had been that Polish Governments must be hostile to Russia. In these circumstances either Poland had been too weak to oppose Germany or had let the Germans come through. Thus Poland had served as a corridor for the German attacks on Russia.

Stalin said Poland's weakness and hostility had been a great source of weakness to the Soviet Union and had permitted the Germans to do what they wished in the East and also in the West since the two were mixed together. It was therefore in Russia's vital interest that Poland should be both strong and friendly. He said there was no intention on the part of the Soviet Union to interfere in Poland's internal affairs, that Poland would live under the parliamentary system, which is like Czechoslovakia, Belgium and Holland, that any talk of an intention to Sovietize Poland was stupid. He said even the Polish leaders, some of whom were communists, were against the Soviet system since the Polish people did not desire collective farms or other aspects of the Soviet system. In this the Polish leaders were right since the Soviet system was not exportable— it must develop from within on the basis of a set of conditions which were not present in Poland. He said that all the Soviet Union wanted was that Poland should not be in a position to open the gates to Germany and in order to prevent this Poland must be strong and democratic.

Stalin then said that before he came to his suggestion as to the practical solution of the question he would like to comment on Mr. Hopkins' remarks concerning future U. S. interests in the world. He said that whether the U. S. wished it or not it was a world power and would have to accept world-wide interests.

Not only this war but the previous war had shown that without U. S. intervention Germany could not have been defeated and that all the events and developments of the last thirty years had confirmed this. In fact the U. S. had more reason to be a world power than any other state. For this reason he fully recognized the right of the U. S. as a world power to participate in the Polish question and that the Soviet interest in Poland did not in any way exclude those of England and the U. S. Mr. Hopkins had spoken of unilateral action in Poland and U. S. public opinion concerning it. It was true that Russia had taken such unilateral action but they had been compelled to.

Stalin recalled that the Soviet Government had recognized the Warsaw Government and concluded a treaty with it at a time when their allies did not recognize this government. These were admittedly unilateral acts which would have been much better left undone but the fact was they had not met with any understanding on the part of their allies. The need for these actions had arisen out of the presence of Soviet troops in Poland and it would have been impossible to have waited until such time as the allies had come to an agreement on Poland. The logic of the war against Germany had demanded that the Soviet rear be assured and the Lublin Committee had been of great assistance to the Red Army at all times and it was for this reason that these actions had been taken by the Soviet Government. He said it was contrary to the Soviet policy to set up a Soviet administration on foreign soil since this would look like occupation and be resented by the local inhabitants.

It was for this reason, Stalin continued, that some Polish administration had to be established in Poland and this could be done only with those who had helped the Red Army. He said he wished to emphasize that these steps had not been taken with any desire to eliminate or exclude Russia's allies. He must point

31

out, however, the Soviet action in Poland had been more successful than British action in Greece and at no time had they
been compelled to undertake the measures which the British
had taken in Greece. Stalin then turned to his suggestion for the
solution of the Polish problem.

Marshal Stalin said that he felt that we should examine the
composition of the future Government of National Unity. He
said there were eighteen or twenty ministries in the present
Polish Government and that four or five of these portfolios could
be given representatives of other Polish groups taken from the
list submitted by Great Britain and the U. S. (Molotov whispered to Stalin who then said he meant four and not five posts
in the government.) He said he thought the Warsaw Poles
would not accept more than four ministers from other democratic groups. [The discussion then turned to personalities, and
Hopkins said he would require some time to consider the
Marshal's suggestion.]

[The third conversation dealt with the Far East and need not
be detailed here since it involved no disagreements. This was
the conversation in which, according to the Bohlen notes, Stalin
declared that "the Soviet people would not be a factor in any
way hindering Chinese unity but on the contrary would help
the Chinese to achieve it. In regard to the Generalissimo the
Marshal said he knew little of any Chinese leader but that he
felt that Chiang Kai-Shek was the best of the lot and would be
the one to undertake the unification of China. He said he saw
no other possible leader and that for example he did not believe
that the Chinese communist leaders were as good or would be
able to bring about the unification of China. . . . In Manchuria
as in any part of China where Soviet troops went the Chinese
administration would be set up under Chiang. . . ." The future
occupation regime for Germany was also discussed. During the

fourth conversation, on May 30, the question of Poland came up again:]

Mr. Hopkins said he would like to continue the discussion on Poland. He said first of all he would like to make a general observation. Historically speaking the people of Russia and, since the revolution, the people of the Soviet Union, had distrusted successive Polish Governments and to some extent the Polish people. Likewise, for many years the Polish people had feared Russia and, since the revolution, the Soviet Union. He said that at their first meeting he had indicated to Marshal Stalin as clearly as he could that the U. S. was not only not interested in the establishment of a *cordon sanitaire* around Russia but on the contrary was aggressively opposed to it; that the U. S. had no economic interests of substantial importance in Poland and that we believed that the U. S., the Soviet Union and England in working to help create a new Polish state that would be friendly to Russia could have an immense moral and political effect in the task of bringing about genuine Polish-Soviet friendship. He said that the Soviet Union alone working directly with Poland would find this a more difficult task and in those circumstances Poland might remain a troublesome and even threatening area for Russia. However, if the three nations genuinely got together and were associated with the creation of a new Polish state, we believed that would have a most helpful effect in the establishment of a friendly and independent Poland which would be genuinely friendly to the Soviet Union.

Marshal Stalin said he agreed. There was no intention on the part of the Soviet Government to exclude her allies England and America from participation in the solution of this problem.

Mr. Hopkins inquired if the Marshal believed it would be a fact that the U. S. and British participation would be helpful.

Marshal Stalin said that undoubtedly the solution would carry more weight if it was tripartite.

Mr. Hopkins said he would like to accent once again the reasons for our concern in regard to Poland, and indeed, in regard to other countries which were geographically far from our borders. He said there were certain fundamental rights which, when infringed upon or denied caused concern in the U. S. These were cardinal elements which must be present if a parliamentary system is to be established and maintained. He said for example:

(1) There must be the right of freedom of speech so that people could say what they wanted to, the right of assembly, the right of movement and the right to worship at any church that they desired;

(2) All political parties, except the fascist party and fascist elements, who represented or could represent democratic governments should be permitted the free use, without distinction, of the press, radio, meetings and other facilities of political expression;

(3) All citizens should have the right of public trial, defense by counsel of their own choosing, and the right of habeas corpus.

He concluded that if we could find a meeting of minds in regard to these general principles which would be the basis for future free elections, then he was sure we could find ways and means to agree on procedures to carry them into effect. He then asked the Marshal if he would care to comment in a general sense or more specifically in regard to the general observations he had made concerning the fundamentals of a new Polish state.

Marshal Stalin replied that these principles of democracy are well known and would find no objection on the part of the Soviet Government. He was sure that the Polish Government, which in its declarations had outlined just such principles, would not only not oppose them but would welcome them. He said, however, that in regard to the specific freedoms mentioned by Mr. Hopkins, they could only be applied in full in peace time, and even then with certain limitations. He said, for example, the fascist party, whose intention it was to overthrow democratic governments, could not be permitted to enjoy to the full extent these freedoms. He said secondly there were the limitations imposed by war. All states when they were threatened by war or their frontiers were not secure had found it necessary to introduce certain restrictions. This had been done in England, France, the Soviet Union and elsewhere and perhaps to a lesser extent in the U. S. which was protected by wide oceans. It was for these reasons that only in time of peace could consideration be given to the full application of these freedoms. For example, he said that in time of war no state will allow the free unrestricted use of radio transmitters which could be used to convey information to the enemy. With reference to freedom of speech, certain restrictions had to be imposed for military security. . . . He said, to sum up: (1) during time of war these political freedoms could not be enjoyed to the full extent, and (2) nor could they apply without reservations to fascist parties trying to overthrow the government. . . .

Mr. Hopkins said he thoroughly understood the Marshal's opinions. He added that when he had left the Crimea Conference President Roosevelt had thought the Polish matter was virtually settled. Mr. Hopkins said he and all the other American representatives thought the same and felt that in very short time Mr. Molotov, Mr. Harriman and Sir Archibald Clark Kerr* would be able to carry out the Crimea Decision. . . . He must confess that he had been bewildered and disturbed that

* The then British ambassador to the Soviet Union.

one thing after another had seemed to occur to prevent the carrying out of the decision which all had thought was clear and sure. . . . Mr. Hopkins said that he must say that rightly or wrongly there was a strong feeling among the American people that the Soviet Union wished to dominate Poland. . . .

[Twice again, during the Hopkins visit, was the question of Poland discussed. The record of the fifth conversation, which concerned the Poles who were to be called to Moscow to "consult" on the formation of the Provisional Government of National Unity, has not yet been published. Hopkins also attempted to persuade Stalin to release fourteen Polish underground leaders who had been arrested by Soviet troops and charged with subversive activities against the Soviet forces. In an after-dinner conversation on June 1, Hopkins according to a memorandum of record[2] "reminded Stalin again of the many minority groups in America who were not sympathetic to the Soviet Union" and told him very forcefully that he must "believe me when I told him that our whole relationship was threatened by the impasse of Poland." Stalin was adamant against release of the arrested Polish leaders, inveighed against alleged British connivance with the Polish Government in Exile in London, and observed that "we must take into consideration Russian opinion as well as American opinion; that it was the Russian forces that had liberated Poland and if they had not gained the victory in Poland, with such a great loss of Russian life, nobody would be talking about a new Poland. . . ."]

———————

NOTES

1. The language of this chapter is taken from the Bohlen notes, first published in Robert E. Sherwood's *Roosevelt and Hopkins* (New York: Harper, 1948) and later officially in Volume I of *Foreign Relations of the United States—Conference of Berlin (Potsdam)* (Washington: Government Printing Office, 1960; hereafter cited as *Potsdam Papers*), pp. 24 ff. Some condensations have been made, so as to focus on the principal issues. Sentences within brackets are condensations, and dots indicate deletions of nonessential detail. In a few cases the grammar of the original, probably hastily written, minutes has been improved.

2. Ibid., p. 57.

3

Poland: Roots of Conflict

Under a secret protocol to the Molotov-Ribbentrop pact of August 23, 1939 Poland was in effect divided between Russia and Germany. "In the event of a territorial and political rearrangement of the areas belonging to the Polish state," the protocol said, "the spheres of influence of Germany and the USSR shall be bounded approximately by the line of the rivers Narew, Vistula, and San."[1] This line of demarcation, subsequently modified by a secret supplementary protocol dated September 28, corresponded in the center to the so-called Curzon Line, which had been proposed in 1919 by the Allied Supreme Council as representing the approximate ethnic boundary between Poles on the one hand and Ukrainians and White Russians on the other. In its northern and southern portions, the demarcation line between Russia and Germany ran to the west of the Curzon Line, i.e., it gave Russia more territory.

As the Polish army was crushed by the German Wehrmacht and its remnants retreated to the east, the Germans encouraged the Russians to attack the Poles from the rear.[2] The German government desired that Russia should occupy its entire sphere of influence in Poland to preclude the continued existence of a Polish rump state in that area.[3] After Poland had thus been divided between them, Germany and Russia concluded a Boundary and Friendship Treaty with a secret supplementary protocol which declared: "Both parties will tolerate in their territories no Polish agitation which affects the territories of the other party. They will suppress in their territories all beginnings of such agitation and inform each other concerning suitable measures for this purpose."[4] Russia annexed its portion of Poland, incorporating it into the Ukrainian and White Russian Soviet Republics. Poland had ceased to exist.

Poland had suffered this fate before, only to rise again. Once a great empire that included most of the Ukraine and White Russia as well as German and Baltic populations, it had been "partitioned" between Russia and Prussia in 1772 and again in 1793. But the Poles rose under Kosciuszko and regained most of their lost territory, only to be decisively defeated in 1795, when the country was divided up between Russia, Prussia, and Austria. However, the Poles never stopped fighting for the reestablishment of their nation. For a while their hopes were pinned on Napoleon, and a Polish army accompanied him against Russia. After Napoleon's defeat, the Congress of Vienna permitted a small "Congress Poland" to exist, but it was placed under the Czar and by 1820 it had become a Russian province. Still the Poles continued to fight for their freedom until a century later, in 1919, a new Polish state once more emerged on the international scene.

The problem of Poland between World War I and World War II was thus how to maintain independence in the face of two covetous neighbors, and the aim of Polish diplomacy was to obtain effective Western guarantees that would deter both Germany and Russia. The peculiar Polish security interests (which were shared by other states bordering on Russia) were the reason why no collective security agreement could be reached between Russia and the West in the face of the Nazi threat in 1939. As Churchill has written: "The obstacle to such an agreement was the terror of these same border countries of receiving Soviet help in the shape of Soviet Armies marching through their territories to defend them from the Germans and incidentally incorporate them in the Soviet-Communist system of which they were the most vehement opponents. Poland, Rumania, Finland and the three Baltic states did not know whether it was German aggression or Russian rescue that they dreaded more. It was this hideous choice that paralyzed British and French policy."[5]

If Poland had ceased to exist after September 1939, there were nevertheless Poles who kept up the fight in accordance with age-old tradition. Thousands of Polish soldiers who had escaped the Nazi-Soviet pincers made their way to the West, as did some distinguished Polish statesmen. On September 30 a Polish government-in-exile was established in France and promptly recognized by France, Great Britain, and, shortly later, the United States. Some 84,000 Polish troops were under arms in France at the time of the debacle there in 1940, and many of them were evacuated to England, as was the Polish government-in-exile. That government came to be known as the London Polish government (as distinguished from the later Lublin government), and it maintained especially close relations with the British government. This was understandable, for it had been Britain's guarantee to Poland which had resulted in its declaration of war against Germany in 1939 when Hitler had sent his Wehrmacht into Poland.

Poland: Roots of Conflict

When Hitler later launched his attack against Russia in 1941, and after Great Britain had concluded a mutual assistance agreement with the Soviet Union, the London Polish govern- ment sought ways and means of establishing relations with the Soviet Union—but it did so as an aggrieved party and in a proud spirit of national assertiveness. As Prime Minister Mikolajczyk has written: "Unlike Britain and the U. S. . . . we had certain conditions to present to the Russians in exchange for our pledge of support. The conditions we offered were generous. We ruled out reparations and indemnities, though entitled to both. We promised to forgive, if not forget. To our astonishment, when we sat down with Russian Ambassador Ivan Maisky in London to draw up a new pact, we learned that Russia was not willing to accept our modest claims."[6] The Polish claims were the re- establishment of Poland in its pre-1939 boundaries. This Russia, even at the time when it was most sorely beset by the German invaders, was unwilling to guarantee.

The Soviet position in the Polish-Soviet negotiations in 1941 was completely inflexible: they regarded their annexation of eastern Poland as final; they claimed that it corresponded to ethnographic realities; they referred to the fact that the British government had in 1920 sponsored a frontier line (the Curzon Line) which was almost the same; and they argued that the ex- perience they were undergoing at the hands of the German army proved how essential these areas were to the defense of the Soviet Union. They were prepared to free Polish prisoners of war in Russia and to permit the formation of a Polish army on Russian soil by recruitment among the released prisoners and other Poles. They were prepared to establish diplomatic rela- tions with the London Polish government, but in the end they were only willing to state publicly, in the agreement with that government, that they regard "the Soviet-German treaties of

41

1939 as to territorial changes in Poland as having lost their validity."

On the public record, this statement seemed to leave the matter of Poland's future eastern frontiers in doubt, but when Polish Prime Minister Sikorski after signing the Polish-Soviet agreement declared that Poland's pre-1939 frontiers should be restored, he received an immediate answer from *Izvestia* (August 3, 1941) to the effect that the Soviet Union had promised nothing in that regard. The British government also confined itself to a declaration that "His Majesty's Government do not recognize any territorial changes which have been effected in Poland since August 1939," and Foreign Minister Eden explained in answer to a question in the House of Commons that this did not involve any British guarantee of Poland's frontiers.[7] The U.S. position was that all territorial questions should be postponed until after the war.[8] This was, in fact, the position of some of the Polish leaders, who felt that a war-weakened Russia would in the end not be able to oppose Polish national aspirations.[9]

Meanwhile, as Polish-Russian relations were formally normalized, the Soviet authorities began to release Polish prisoners of war in Russia, but it turned out that the only Poles who were made available for service in a new Polish army on Russian soil were those who came from western Poland, plus ethnic Poles from eastern Poland (i.e., excluding Ukrainians, White Russians, and Jews from the latter area). Although Stalin agreed with General Sikorski, the Polish Prime Minister, that six or seven Polish divisions were to be formed in Russia, the Poles quickly noted that most of the officers who were known to have fallen into Russian captivity were not among the soldiers being released from prisoner-of-war camps. Since the new Polish divisions were to be equipped with American arms, and since the supply situation was terribly strained, the Polish divisions were very slow in being formed.

On every occasion of contact with Western leaders, Stalin pressed for recognition of eastern frontiers that would extend Russian territory after the war. When Foreign Minister Eden visited Moscow in December 1941, Stalin offered assurances of Russian support for a privileged British security position in western Europe in return for British recognition of the Soviet boundaries roughly as they had been before the German attack. When Molotov was in London in May 1942 to conclude a mutual assistance treaty with Great Britain, he pressed hard for British recognition of the Russian position and would have obtained it but for American objections.[10] (Churchill considered that such an extension of Russian frontiers to where they had been at the time of the Nazi attack would be compatible with the Atlantic Charter.[11]) In January 1943 the Soviet government informed the Polish government-in-exile that henceforth those refugees in Russia who had come from the former eastern provinces of Poland would be treated as Soviet citizens. The Polish government-in-exile, of course, protested this pronouncement as illegal and unacceptable.

Meanwhile, the position of the nascent new Polish army in Russia became more and more difficult. In October 1941 the London Polish government addressed a note to the Soviet ambassador expressing disquiet about the whereabouts of "several thousand Polish officers who have not returned to Poland and who have not been found in Soviet military camps." The Russian ambassador's reply, one month later, was to the effect that all Polish officers on the territory of the U. S. S. R. had been set free.[12] In November 1941, the Polish ambassador in Moscow obtained an audience with Stalin and raised, more specifically,

43

the question of what had happened to approximately 15,000 Polish officers and noncoms who were known to have been in camps at Starobielsk, Kozielsk, and Ostashkov. The Polish underground had knowledge that those prisoners had been transferred from their camps in early 1940 to an unknown destination, but only between 350 and 400 had reported to the Polish army in Russia. Stalin replied that the Russian "amnesty" knew no exceptions, and he declined to discuss the matter further. In December 1941 General Sikorski flew to Moscow and put the same question to Stalin at a time when the Germans were pressing at the very gates of Moscow. Stalin insisted that the Polish officers had been liberated and suggested that they might be "somewhere in Manchuria."[13]

As the supply situation of the Polish army became more difficult, it was arranged that the Polish troops should be permitted to leave Russia through Iran to join the Allied forces in the Middle East. In the course of his discussions of the modalities of that withdrawal, the Polish commander-in-chief, General Anders, had an interview with Stalin in March 1942, when he again raised the question of the missing Polish officers. According to a record of this conversation, Anders said: "Many of our people are still in prisons and labor camps. Only recently released prisoners are reporting all the time. So far, not a single officer removed from Kozielsk, Starobielsk or Ostashkov has turned up. You certainly must have them. We have collected additional information about them. Where can they be?" Stalin replied: "I have already given all necessary orders that they are to be freed. They say they are even in Franz Joseph Land, but there is no one there. I don't know where they are. Why should we retain them? Perhaps they were in camps in territories which were taken over by the Germans and were dispersed."[14] The Poles immediately explained that this was impossible since they were in contact with the underground in Poland itself and would have heard if some of the missing officers had turned up there.

The London Polish government had, in fact, excellent information about the former inmates of the three prisoner-of-war camps as they not only represented the bulk of the Polish officer corps but included political leaders, lawyers, physicians, scientists, and clergymen—the cream of the Polish leadership elements. At Ostashkov there had been between 6,500 and 6,600 officers, many of them reservists who in private life had held important civil posts; at Starobielsk most of the 4,000 prisoners had been noncoms; while at Kozielsk there had been 4,500 personnel of various military ranks, including some of Poland's highest ranking officers, as well as some civilians. According to information available to the London Polish government, Lavrenty Beria, the head of the Soviet secret police, had declared to some Polish representatives as early as the spring of 1940 that in regard to the missing officers, "a great mistake had been made."[15] The London Polish government thus had every reason to suspect that the former occupants of the three prison camps, from whom all news had ceased since early 1940, had been the victims of foul play. But they did not know what kind of foul play it had been.

On April 13, 1943 the German radio announced that on the basis of information furnished by the local population, the German authorities had found in the forest of Katyn near Smolensk "the spot where in secret mass executions, the Bolsheviks murdered 10,000 Polish officers." German authorities, the broadcast said, had found a pit 28 meters long and 16 meters wide in which, twelve deep, lay the bodies of 3,000 Polish officers. In full uniform, and in some cases shackled, all had wounds from pistol bullets in the back of the neck. The Germans said that "search and discovery of other pits were continuing." In a calculated expression of horror, they called for an on-the-spot investigation by the International Red Cross. Two days afterward, the Soviet news agency Tass rejected the German revelation as a dastardly provocation and for the first time gave an explanation of what was supposed to have happened to the missing prisoners: "The Polish prisoners in question," the Soviet story went, "were interned in the vicinity of Smolensk in special camps and were employed in road construction. It was impossible to evacuate them at the time of the approach of the German troops, and as a result they fell into their hands. If, therefore, they have been found murdered, it means they have been murdered by the Germans who for reasons of provocation claim now that the crime has been committed by the Soviet authorities."[16]

The London Polish government was placed in an exceedingly difficult position by the German propaganda campaign. Although nauseated by the German effort to derive propaganda advantage by embroiling Polish relations with the Soviet Union, it felt that it could not ignore the allegations. On April 16 the London Polish government thus issued a statement detailing the known facts about the missing prisoners and about its unsuccessful efforts to obtain an accounting from the Soviet government, and asked that "the facts alleged be verified by a competent international body, such as the International Red Cross." It announced that it had already approached that organization "with a view to their sending a delegation to the place where the massacre of the Polish prisoners of war is said to have taken place."[17] In the view of one eminent historian of Russia's relations with the West, "it is hard, in retrospect, to see how the Poles could have done less."[18]

The Soviet reaction to the Polish statement was exceedingly violent. Stalin informed Churchill and Roosevelt that he intended to break (he used the word "interrupt") relations with the London Polish government for having "struck a treacherous blow at the Soviet Union to help Hitler tyranny" and he claimed that "the fact that the anti-Soviet campaign has been started simultaneously in the German and Polish press and follows identical lines is indubitable evidence of contact and collusion between Hitler—the allies' enemy—and the Sikorski Government in this hostile campaign." In vain did Churchill and Roosevelt urge Stalin to withhold action. They deplored the Polish government's action, but both pointed out that the London Poles were certainly not trying to help Hitler. Roosevelt cabled Stalin: "Incidentally, I have several million Poles in the U. S., a great many of whom are in the Army and Navy. I can assure you that all of them are bitter against the Hitlerites. However, the over-all situation would not be helped by the knowledge of a complete diplomatic break between the Soviet and Polish Governments." Churchill also warned that "public announcement of a break would do the greatest possible harm in the U. S., where the Poles are numerous and influential." However, Stalin broke relations with the London Polish government even before these messages reached him, claiming that "Soviet public opinion was deeply outraged by such conduct, and hence the Soviet government could no longer defer action."[19]

The breakdown of relations between the Polish government in London and the Soviet government was a disaster for the Western allies. In Russia an organization called the "Union of Polish Patriots in the USSR" came to the fore with a declaration denouncing the London Polish government, and it was obvious that that pro-Communist group was being groomed to take over in Poland when Soviet forces reached Polish soil. To make matters worse, General Sikorski, who had been both prime minister and commander-in-chief of the Polish armed forces, was

47

killed in an airplane crash in July 1943. His successor, Stanislaw Mikolajczyk, was an able and moderate political leader who had to harness together a number of differing political tendencies plus the Polish military. It must be remembered that the Polish government in London sponsored not only some 150,000 Polish troops in the Mediterranean and the Middle East but also a Polish Air Force in England and, last but not least, an important underground network in Poland (called the Polish Home Army). The Poles in London were in close contact with the underground. Ominously, they began to receive reports of Polish pro-Communist partisans who were being parachuted into Poland by the Russians.

The United States generally left the lead to the British in the efforts to restore Polish-Russian relations. Roosevelt toyed with the idea of a compromise on the territorial issue involving modification of the Curzon Line that would give the city of Lwow to Poland and "a plebiscite . . . after the shell shock of war had subsided."[20] In general, however, the position of the United States remained that territorial issues should await the peace conference.[21] The British, on the other hand, felt that the sooner the territorial question was settled, the better were the chances that the Russians would acquiesce in a free Poland. A joint U. S.-British demarche in Moscow in September to patch up Soviet-Polish relations met with uncompromising Russian opposition. When Eden, before the Moscow Conference of October 1943, asked Mikolajczyk to empower him to discuss the frontier question with the Russians, the Polish premier flatly refused, reminding Eden of the principles expressed in the Atlantic Charter and warning that if the West bargained away Poland's eastern territories, "it would be only the beginning of Russian demands."[22]

The Polish position prior to the Moscow Conference was set

forth in detail to both Hull and Eden. It asked the American and British governments to guarantee Poland's independence, integrity, and security. Ambassador Ciechanowski told Hull that "anxious to maintain good Polish-Soviet relations in the future, my government would deem undesirable either temporary or partial occupation of Polish territories by the Soviet armies. However, if such occupation were unavoidable as a result of military operations against Germany, it should be dependent on a previous Polish-Soviet understanding, based on the reestablishment of diplomatic relations." The right of the Polish government to administer the country should be guaranteed, and "to safeguard such a guarantee, American-British troops . . . should enter and be stationed on the territory of Poland to protect the population against eventual Soviet reprisals and the creation of accomplished facts."[23] This position, of course, left no room whatever for compromise.

At the Moscow Conference, the Polish question was thus only briefly discussed. Litvinov denounced the London Polish government; declared that the Poles must learn to live as a small national state within their "correct" boundaries, and give up the idea that they were a great power; and asserted that when their interests collided with Russia's interests, they would have to give way. Molotov listened to Eden's plea that the Polish-Russian quarrel be ended, but indicated that he thought the question one for the Soviet government to settle; he affirmed that the Soviet government wanted to see an "independent" Poland; but its government would have to be "friendly" to the Soviet Union, and the group in London was decidedly not. Hull confined his intervention to generalities.[24] The entry made in the final Protocol of the Conference said merely about this item of the agenda that "an exchange of views took place."

On the other hand, the Conference spent a great deal of time on the Four-Power Declaration, which set forth certain principles that would govern the policies of the signatories during the remainder of the war. Paragraph six of that Declaration, in the original American proposal, read: "That they will not employ their military forces within the territories of other states except for the purposes envisaged in this Declaration and after joint consultation *and agreement*." Molotov objected to the words "and agreement" and made it clear that while Russia was willing to consult, it was not willing to submit to a veto over action.[25] Accordingly, the Declaration was issued without the words "and agreement" (see page viii). The Moscow Four-Power Declaration was subsequently hailed as the harbinger of a new era of international understanding because it recorded agreement on "the necessity of establishing . . . a general international organization, based on the principle of the sovereign equality of all peace-loving states," but it did not advance the solution of the questions of Russia's western boundaries and Russia's relations with its neighbor states in Europe.

Cordell Hull nevertheless said, when he reviewed the accomplishments of the Moscow Conference before Congress in November 1943: "As the provisions of the Four-Nation Declaration are carried into effect, there will no longer be need for spheres of influence, for alliances, for balance of power, or any other of the special arrangements through which, in the unhappy past, the nations strove to safeguard their security or to promote their interests." He reasoned that "in the atmosphere of mutual understanding and confidence which made possible [the movement toward an international organization] in Moscow, many of the problems which are difficult today will, as time goes on, undoubtedly become more possible of satisfactory solution through frank and friendly discussion."[26]

The London Polish government did not share this optimistic

interpretation of the meeting, and it concentrated all its efforts to assure that the Western allies would support its uncompromising position at the forthcoming meeting of heads of state at Tehran. The Polish ambassador to the United States handed Hull a memorandum which threatened that, if Soviet troops entered Polish territory without previous resumption of Polish-Soviet relations, the Polish government would "undertake political action against this violation of Polish sovereignty, while the Polish local administration and army in Poland would have to continue to work underground." In London, Mikolajczyk warned that "decisions taken without full consultation with the Polish government upon which the underground in Poland staked its hopes would undoubtedly lead to a serious crisis in that quarter, would create a crisis in Polish circles in England and the Middle East, and might have serious repercussions among Americans of Polish origin."[27] In other words, the London Polish government was threatening that in the event Russian troops entered Poland without its consent, the Polish underground would fight the Russians, and it threatened that if the United States made an agreement with Russia over the head of the Polish government, the latter would mobilize Polish opinion in the United States against the U. S. government.

At the Tehran Conference, Stalin raised the idea that Poland's Western frontier should include an enormous chunk of German territory up to the river Oder, and Churchill readily fell in with that suggestion. Churchill reports that he said to Stalin: "I have no power from Parliament nor, I believe, has the President, to define any frontier lines. But we might now, in Teheran, see if the three heads of governments, working in agreement, could form some sort of policy which we could recommend to the Poles and advise them to accept."[28] There ensued a prolonged discussion of the proposed future frontiers for the Polish state, in which Roosevelt sat by silently. In the end, although the exact modifications of the Curzon Line still were not precisely agreed, Churchill and Stalin agreed that the new Poland should go roughly from the Curzon Line to the Oder.

At a separate, private meeting with Stalin, Roosevelt explained the reason why he did not feel he could commit himself. He told the Soviet dictator that there were six or seven million Americans of Polish extraction who constituted an important voting bloc and whose opinions had to be taken seriously in determining American foreign policy.[29] He referred to the forthcoming electoral campaign in 1944 and, according to the Bohlen memo of that conversation, indicated that "personally he agreed with the views of Marshal Stalin as to the necessity of the restoration of a Polish state but would like to see the eastern border moved farther to the west and the western border moved even to the River Oder. He hoped, however, that the Marshal would understand that for political reasons outlined above, he could not participate in any decision here in Tehran or even next winter on this subject and that he could not publicly take part in any such arrangement at the present time." Roosevelt also appears to have spoken about the desirability of the city of Lwow going to Poland, although the record of this aspect of the confidential conversation is unclear.[30] (In another private talk at Tehran, when the prospective world peace organization was discussed, the President remarked that American naval and air forces could be used to help police the world, but any land armies needed to quell aggression would have to be provided by Russia and Britain.[31])

It was thus left to Churchill to attempt to get the London Polish government to accept a territorial settlement along the lines discussed at Tehran. The matter had become especially urgent because the Red Army was about to reach the old boundary of Poland. But the Poles were adamant: on January 4, 1944, the day when the Red Army crossed the line, Mikolajczyk in a broadcast reaffirmed the order given to the Polish underground to cooperate with the Soviet commanders "if relations [with the London Polish government] should be resumed"; demanded "respect for the rights and interests of the Polish Republic"; invoked the Atlantic Charter and the Four Freedoms; and announced that a delegate of the government had been empowered to act in its name in Poland "to carry out all the functions of the government concerning home administration."[32] The Russian reply, in equally uncompromising terms, denounced the "emigrant" Polish government as incapable of conducting friendly relations with the Soviet Union or of leading an active fight against the Germans in Poland; declared that it wished to see a strong and independent Poland with which it could be friendly; insisted that the eastern boundary, while it need not follow the 1939 line, must correspond to the ethnic situation; and only offered the Poles compensation in the West, "through incorporation with Poland of ancient Polish lands previously wrested by Germany." Pointedly, the Russian statement referred to the "Union of Polish Patriots in the USSR" and announced that a Polish Army Corps under its auspices was operating hand in hand with the Red Army in the battle for liberation.

Churchill was tough with Milolajczyk when he saw him on January 20. "The British Government takes the view that Poland must be strong, independent, and free," he began, and then quickly added, "from the Curzon Line to the Oder." In the premier's own words:

> . . . when I raised the first of my objections about this obvious unilateral partition of Poland, Churchill reminded me a bit tartly that the Anglo-Polish alliance pact, signed just before the outbreak of the war, had obliged Britain to de-

53

fend Poland and Poland's independence against the Germans but had not mentioned the eastern frontiers of Poland. "You must understand this, Mr. Mikolajczyk, Great Britain and the U.S. will not go to war to defend the eastern frontiers of Poland. If an agreement is reached now about those frontiers, this agreement could be guaranteed by Great Britain as well as the Soviet Union. It is not possible under the American Constitution for President Roosevelt to guarantee the frontiers of any foreign country. Therefore, I urge you to agree to the Curzon Line as the eastern frontier of Poland, in principle at least. . . . If you do not act quickly, I cannot be responsible for anything that might take place."[33]

The Polish government felt that it had to obtain the views of the underground before replying to the British initiative. Meanwhile, it tried to mobilize the support of the United States but obtained only an evasive reply. However, Ambassador Harriman in Moscow tried to exercise a moderating influence, and he reported that he felt an agreement was still possible if the Polish government would drop its most outspokenly anti-Soviet members and if it at least tacitly accepted the Soviet position on boundaries.[34] But the Polish underground was, if anything, more proudly unyielding than its government. It was willing to accept the German territory offered in the west, but refused to cede what was asked in the east and even objected to the acquisition of German territory (East Prussia) by Russia. It was willing, on the other hand, to accept a temporary line of demarcation but one substantially to the east of what Russia proposed. And it affirmed that changes in the Polish government and high command could not be made "in obedience to the demands of a foreign power." The Polish troops in the Mediterranean theatre took an equally unyielding position.[35] Mikolajczyk's reply to Churchill was therefore wholly negative.

Poland: Roots of Conflict

While the American government continued to maintain silence in the matter, Churchill on February 22, 1944 made a statement in the House of Commons in which he recalled that the British government had never guaranteed any particular boundary of Poland and had, in fact, not approved the Polish occupation of certain territories to the east of the Curzon Line in 1920 (when the Polish army under Pilsudski had beaten the Red Army). He went on to say: "I have an intense sympathy with the Poles, that heroic race whose national spirit centuries of misfortune cannot quench, but I also have sympathy with the Russian standpoint. Twice in our lifetime Russia has been violently assaulted by Germany. . . . Russia has the right to reassurance against future attacks from the West, and we are going all the way with her to see that she gets it, not only by the might of her arms but by the approval and assent of the United Nations."

The London Polish government immediately protested this speech. Mikolajczyk repeatedly attempted to obtain a hearing from Roosevelt, but the President sent him a letter stating that he wanted to see him very much "but a visit at this time may bring misunderstanding in public opinion."[36] When the Polish premier finally succeeded in seeing Roosevelt in June, it was on condition that he would make no public statement. The meeting was amiable. The President ventilated the possibility of a compromise on the boundary question and urged the Polish premier to visit Stalin. Mikolajczyk agreed to see Stalin. But a message from Roosevelt to the Soviet dictator, suggesting such a meeting, met with a negative response since Mikolajczyk made it clear to the Soviet ambassador in London that he refused to reorganize his government or to make any territorial concessions.

The Western invasion of Europe was now imminent, while

55

in the east the Russian offensive had come to a halt. Meanwhile, the Polish question was further complicated by the fact that the Russians seemed about to set up a rival Polish government. However, the American government did not feel that it could afford to press the Russians too strongly. The landings in Normandy, as Cordell Hull has written, "had to be coordinated with Russian military movements in the East so that the Germans could not draw off too large a portion of their forces to meet us in the West. We could not afford to become partisan in the Polish question to the extent of alienating Russia at that crucial moment."[37] The Russians, as it turned out, kept the word they had given at Tehran by launching a major offensive with 130 divisions after the Western Allies had landed in France. While that offensive heartened the Allied military leaders, its momentum was such that it carried the Red Army for the first time into territory that the Russians themselves had recognized as Polish, thereby creating a new crisis in Polish-Russian relations.

Now it was Churchill's turn to ask Stalin to receive Mikolajczyk. Stalin replied that, since Russia did not wish to set up a Russian administration in Poland, and since "we have not found in Poland other forces capable of establishing a Polish administration," he was getting in touch with the Polish Committee of National Liberation which had been established at Lublin and which "intended" to set up such an administration. However, he would not refuse to see Mikolajczyk.[38] With great difficulty, the British government managed to persuade the Polish premier to go, but while he was on his way the Russian government signed an agreement with the Lublin group, entrusting it with the administration of the Polish liberated territory. When Mikolajczyk arrived in Moscow, preceded by messages from Churchill and Roosevelt urging reconciliation, he was coldly received. Molotov asked him why he had come. Stalin repeated the well-known Russian position on frontiers but suggested that if Mikolajczyk's group reached an accord with the Committee of National Liberation, some small changes to the benefit of the Poles might be made in the Curzon Line. While Russia had not yet recognized the Lublin group as a Polish government, Stalin was suggesting that the London Polish government could be recognized by Russia only if it accepted some if not all the members of the Lublin group, i.e., if it formed a coalition with them.

Mikolajczyk saw Stalin on August 3, 1944. On August 1 the Polish Home Army in Warsaw had risen against the Germans in expectation of freeing it before the Red Army reached the city. The anti-Communist Poles in Warsaw were of course not in touch with the Russian command, but they had decided that the time had come to strike because the city's suburbs on the eastern bank of the Vistula were already under Russian artillery fire and the Polish radio station in Moscow had called on the people of Warsaw to rise against the Germans.[39] The Polish underground in Warsaw was soon opposed by five picked German divisions and it was clear that the fate of the uprising depended on the speed of the Russian advance into the city. The Russian troops, however, arraigned themselves on the eastern bank of the Vistula to the north and south of Warsaw and marked time. The embattled Poles in Warsaw had food and ammunition only for about a week's fighting, and soon they pleaded in messages to London for supplies and for relief. Mikolajczyk in Moscow and Churchill in telegrams from London besought Stalin to help, but Stalin replied evasively, expressing doubt that a major uprising had taken place but promising some assistance. Molotov claimed that the Germans were counterattacking the Russian troops.

In the absence of any Russian assistance to the uprising in

57

Warsaw, the R. A. F. started dropping supplies from planes based in Italy, but its losses during these long trips were prohibitive and the flights had to be stopped. Mikolajczyk appealed to the U. S. Air Force, which had run a shuttle service between bases in Britain and Russia, to drop supplies to the Warsaw fighters. But when the United States asked for permission for its planes to land behind the Russian lines, Vyshinsky replied: "The Soviet Government cannot of course object to English or American aircraft dropping arms in the region of Warsaw, since this is an American and British affair. But they decidedly object to American or British aircraft, after dropping arms in the region of Warsaw, landing on Soviet territory, since the Soviet government do not wish to associate themselves either directly or indirectly with the adventure in Warsaw." In a message to Churchill, Stalin declared that he had become "convinced that the Warsaw action represents a reckless and terrible adventure which is costing the population large sacrifices. . . . In the situation which has arisen the Soviet command has come to the conclusion that it must dissociate itself from the Warsaw adventure, as it cannot take either direct or indirect responsibility for the Warsaw action."[40]

For sixty-three days the Poles in Warsaw kept up the fight against towering odds while Churchill and Roosevelt appealed to Stalin to come to their assistance. Meanwhile, Mikolajczyk, who had returned to London, was desperately trying to work out a political compromise which might save the lives of the remaining embattled freedom fighters. He told Churchill that he was prepared to offer the Lublin Committee fourteen seats, but his offer met with no response from Moscow. Churchill proposed to Roosevelt that American planes be sent over Warsaw with instructions to land behind the Russian lines even without Russian consent, but Roosevelt felt this would only create a major crisis with the Russians. Churchill seems to have agreed, for he later wrote that he "should have liked to say, 'we are sending our aeroplanes to land in your territory, after delivering supplies to Warsaw. If you do not treat them properly, all convoys will be stopped from this moment by us.' But the reader of these pages in after-years must realise that everyone always has to keep in mind the fortunes of millions of men fighting in a worldwide struggle, and that terrible and even humbling submissions must at times be made to the general aim."[41]

After the battle had gone on for six weeks, the Russians changed their tactics and began to give some artillery and air support to the Polish Home Army in Warsaw. Also some Polish troops under Russian command were ferried across the Vistula and tried to join up with the fighting within the city, but they suffered great losses and the survivors had to be brought back. Russian landing fields were made available and one large flight of American bombers was thus able to drop supplies, on September 18, but it was too late. On October 2, after a last broadcast in which they called down God's judgment on those responsible for their betrayal, the Polish forces in Warsaw ceased resistance. Of the 40,000 men and women of the underground army, about 15,000 had been killed. The German army lost 10,000 dead in the battle, and 9,000 wounded. The proportions, as Churchill suggests, attest to the bitter, hand-to-hand character of the fighting. When the Russians entered the city three months later, they found little but shattered streets and the unburied dead.

As one historian summed up the situation:

> The crisis in Polish affairs which had thus developed in the first part of August deserves a place in the history of the Second World War like that which Thucydides gave to the Athenian attack on Melos. The affair had all the elements

of tragedy, not only for Poland but for the world at large. Stalin's cold-blooded decision to destroy the Polish Home Army, to deprive the London Government of all effective power in Polish affairs, and to disregard the feelings of the population of Poland herself meant sacrificing much of the sympathy of the British and American public in favour of what he believed to be the security of his western frontier. Polish nationalism and folly had helped to bring the disaster to its climax; Russian brutality and ruthlessness, Roosevelt's failure to make his opinion about the Curzon Line clear to the Poles, and the bloodthirst of German revenge all united to make this passage of Polish history into unmitigated tragedy.[42]

The rest of the story between the fall of Warsaw and the Yalta Conference is quickly told. Churchill was in Moscow in October 1944 to discuss a whole range of difficulties that had accumulated in eastern Europe. At that conference, Roosevelt was unable to participate because of the election campaign. Churchill brought with him a proposal drawn up by Mikolajczyk which called for the formation of a Polish government in which the Communists would have one-fifth of the posts. On the territorial question, the proposal was ambiguous. Churchill urged Stalin to discuss the matter with the Polish premier, and when Stalin agreed he summoned Mikolajczyk urgently to Moscow. The discussion got nowhere as Mikolajczyk still refused to accept the Curzon Line. At one point Molotov intervened in the argument to remark that at Tehran all the Big Three had agreed on the Curzon Line as the proper frontier for the new Poland. (Ambassador Harriman subsequently rectified this impression by pointing out that Roosevelt had not participated in the discussions at Tehran on Poland's western frontier.) Again and again, Churchill attempted to bring the Polish and Russian points of view closer together, but each time he was rebuffed by one side or by both.[43] In the end, Stalin told Mikolajczyk to talk with the Lublin Committee. These pro-Communist Poles now claimed 75 per cent of the posts in any Polish government. In a final talk, Stalin made it clear that if Mikolajczyk were to form a government acceptable to Russia, the Lublin Poles must have a majority.[44]

In their extremity, the Poles in London again turned to the United States. It was now October, less than a month before the 1944 elections, and Roosevelt was fearful that a row over Poland could alienate the important Polish vote, especially in the Middle West. Particularly embarrassing was Mikolajczyk's reference to Molotov's claim that the American President had agreed to the Curzon Line a year before at the Tehran Conference. The President thus temporized while he tried to mend his fences with the Polish-American Congress, which was becoming restive.[45] Not until after he had been re-elected, on November 17, did he reply to Mikolajczyk in a letter delivered by Ambassador Harriman. The letter was as evasive as the U. S. reply to a similar plea in January: it declared that the U. S. government stood "unequivocally for a strong, free and independent Polish state with the untrammeled right of the Polish people to order their internal existence as they see fit"; but on the critical frontier question it offered no specific support, stating merely that if mutual agreement on the subject were reached between the Polish, Soviet, and British governments, the United States "would offer no objection." While the United States could not give any guarantee of specific frontiers, Roosevelt concluded, the prospective world organization would assure the inviolability of agreed frontiers.[46]

Within the London Polish government, there were some who felt that some concessions on the territorial issue were inevitable, but they were in a minority. There was extensive discussion whether some modification of the Curzon Line, notably through inclusion of the city of Lwow, might be negotiated with American help. Ambassador Harriman indicated to Mikolajczyk that he was prepared to talk along such lines with Stalin. But the parties represented in the government-in-exile, with the exception of Mikolajczyk's own Peasant Party, were all opposed to the suggestion. The Polish premier thus resigned his office on November 24. The succeeding government under Tomasz Arciszewski was even more unyielding than the previous one. It was clear that the Russians would now soon proclaim the Lublin group to be the legal government of Poland. President Roosevelt sent a message to Stalin asking him to stay his hand, but the message, dated December 20, was not strongly worded.[47] At the time when it was sent, the German Rundstedt offensive had just broken the American lines in the Ardennes and on December 18 Nazi panzer units had forged to within eight miles of the headquarters of the First U. S. Army.[48]

In a long debate on the Polish question in the House of Commons, Churchill was unsparing in his criticism of the London Poles. He explained that Mikolajczyk had resigned because he was "confronted with the obstinate and inflexible resistance of his London colleagues, whose veto was like the former *Liberum Veto,* which played so great a part in the ruin of Poland." Since Mikolajczyk's resignation, the Polish government had, he said, "been almost entirely reconstituted in a form which in some respects I certainly am not able to applaud." He predicted that because of the failure of the Polish government, troubles would arise between the Russians and the Polish underground as the Red Army advanced through Poland. Churchill defended the British government's support for the Soviet claim to the Curzon Line, including the claim that the territory of Lwow should be assigned to the Soviet Union. The Prime Minister also expressed his regret that various factors in the domestic situation in the United States had made it impossible for the position of that government to be stated with precision.[49]

On December 31, 1944 the Lublin Committee constituted itself as the Provisional National Government of the Polish Republic. On January 5, 1945 the Soviet government—overriding a final appeal by President Roosevelt—recogized the Provisional Government. On January 17 Stalin announced that the Red Army, together with the First Polish Army, had liberated Warsaw, and on the following day, members of the Provisional Government entered the city to establish themselves upon the rubble and ashes to which it had been reduced during the tragic uprising of August and September. Meanwhile, the U. S. and British governments continued to recognize the London Polish government. This was the situation when the Big Three met in Yalta in early February 1945.

NOTES

1. Department of State, *Documents on German Foreign Policy, 1918-1945,* Series D, Volume VII, pp. 246/247 (Document 229).

2. ". . . Please discuss this at once with Molotov and see if the Soviet Union does not consider it desirable for Russian forces to move at the proper time against Polish forces in the Russian sphere of interest and, for their part, occupy this territory." Telegram from Reich Foreign Minister to the German Ambassador in the Soviet Union, September 3, 1939. Ibid., pp. 540/541 (Document 567).

3. ". . . From the communication made to you by Molotov on September 14, we assume that the Soviet Government will take a hand militarily, and that it intends to begin its operations now. We wel-

come this. The Soviet Government thus relieves us of the necessity of annihilating the remainder of the Polish Army by pursuing it as far as the Russian boundary. Also the question is disposed of in case a Russian intervention did not take place, or whether in the area lying to the east of the German zone of influence a political vacuum might not occur. Since we on our part have no intention of undertaking any political or administrative activities in these areas, apart from what is made necessary by military operations, without such an intervention on the part of the Soviet Government there might be the possibility of the construction of new states there." Telegram from Reich Foreign Minister Ribbentrop to the German Ambassador in the Soviet Union, September 15, 1939. Stalin agreed wholeheartedly that anything that in the future might create friction between Germany and the Soviet Union must be avoided. From this point of view, he told the German Ambassador, "he considered it wrong to leave an independent Polish rump state." Department of State, *Documents on German Foreign Policy, 1918-1945,* Series D, Volume VIII, pp. 68-69 (Document 70) and p. 130 (Document 131).

4. Ibid., p. 166 (Document 160). A piquant footnote to this macabre chapter of history is found in the explanation that the Russians originally proposed to give for their invasion and annexation of eastern Poland. According to a telegram from the German ambassador in Moscow dated September 16, 1939, Molotov proposed that the Soviet Union issue a communiqué which would explain that since the Polish state had collapsed, all agreements concluded with Poland were void; that third powers might try to profit from the chaos which had arisen; and that the Soviet Union therefore considered itself obligated to intervene "to protect its Ukrainian and White Russian brothers and make it possible for these unfortunate people to work in peace." Molotov added rather ingenuously that, while the proposed statement was "jarring to German sensibilities . . . the Soviet Government unfortunately saw no possibility of any other motivation, since the Soviet Union had thus far not concerned itself about the plight of its minorities in Poland and had to justify abroad, in some way or other, its present intervention." As the Germans would not agree, a joint communiqué was later issued which did not mention Ukrainians or White Russians in eastern Poland. Ibid., pp. 44, 76, 96 (Documents 46, 78, 94).

5. Winston Churchill, *The Second World War* (Boston: Houghton Mifflin, 1948-1953). I: *The Gathering Storm* (1948). II: *Their Finest Hour* (1949). III: *The Grand Alliance* (1950). IV: *The Hinge of Fate* (1950). V: *Closing the Ring* (1951). VI: *Triumph and Tragedy* (1953). From *The Gathering Storm*, p. 362.

6. Stanislaw Mikolajczyk, *The Rape of Poland—Pattern of Soviet Aggression* (New York: McGraw-Hill, 1948), p. 16.

7. Royal Institute of International Affairs, *America, Britain, and Russia—Their Cooperation and Conflict, 1941-1946*, by William Hardy McNeill (London: Oxford University Press, 1953), p. 47.

8. *The Memoirs of Cordell Hull* (New York: Macmillan, 1948), II, 1166.

9. Prime Minister Sikorski is himself reported to have expressed the view that "the question of the Polish borders will be settled by the correlation of forces after the war." David J. Dallin, *Soviet Russia's Foreign Policy, 1939-1942* (New Haven: Yale University Press, 1942), p. 399.

10. The strongly negative U.S. reaction was described by Cordell Hull as follows: "We indicated that, if the treaty in its proposed form were signed, we might not be able to remain silent since silence might give tacit consent. On the contrary we might have to issue a separate statement clearly stating that we did not subscribe to its principles and clauses. This would be a sharp break within the United Nations, on this point at least, but there was no other course we could logically pursue." Hull *Memoirs*, II, 1172.

11. Prior to Molotov's visit, Churchill told Roosevelt on April 23, 1942: "The increasing gravity of the war has led me to feel that the principles of the Atlantic Charter ought not to be construed so as to deny Russia the frontiers she occupied when Germany attacked her. This was the basis on which Russia acceded to the Charter. . . . I hope therefore that you will be able to give us a free hand to sign the treaty which Stalin desires as soon as possible. Everything portends an immense renewal of the German invasion of Russia in the spring, and there is very little we can do to help the only country that is heavily engaged with the German armies. . . ." Churchill, *The Hinge of Fate*, p. 327.

12. Mikolajczyk, pp. 20-21.

13. Ibid., p. 22. Some historians regard this conversation, which

took place when Russia's military fortunes were at their lowest ebb, as having represented the best opportunity for a compromise between Russian and Polish territorial aspirations. Stalin raised the boundary issue with Sikorski not in terms of the Curzon Line but in terms of "a little" change. Mikolajczyk (p. 23) reports that Stalin referred to "very slight frontier alterations." According to W. W. Kulski in *Foreign Affairs,* July 1947 ("The Lost Opportunity for Russian-Polish Friendship"), Stalin added that he would not in any case claim the town of Lwow, which was ethnically Polish. In the opinion of Herbert Feis, "it may be that at this time the Polish government missed its best chance to win some measure of compromise from the Soviet government. Russian powers of resistance were being most exhaustively tried. Friendship and support in war probably meant more to the Soviet rulers just then than ever again." Herbert Feis, *Churchill, Roosevelt, Stalin—The War They Waged and the Peace They Sought* (Princeton, N.J.: Princeton University Press, 1957), pp. 33-34.

14. Record of Anders-Stalin conversation of March 18, 1942, *Katyn Forest Massacre* (see chap. 1, note 9), p. 961.

15. Ibid., p. 554; Mikolajczyk, p. 36.

16. This has been the Russian side of the story ever since. After the Red Army reoccupied the Smolensk area, the Soviet government appointed a "Special Commission for Ascertaining the Circumstances of the Shooting of Polish Officer Prisoners by the German Fascist Invaders in the Katyn Forest." The complete record is included in *Katyn Forest Massacre.* Thus the Russians produced a camp commander named Vetoshnikov who testified that "communications with Smolensk were cut. Then I myself with several staff members went to Smolensk to clarify the situation. . . . I applied to the chief of traffic of the Smolensk section of the Western Railway, Ivanov, asking him to provide the camp with railway cars for the evacuation of the Polish prisoners. But Ivanov answered that I could not count on receiving cars. I also tried to get in touch with Moscow to obtain permission to set out on foot, but I failed." An engineer Ivanov was also produced, who testified that "the administration of the Polish war prisoner camp applied to my office for cars for evacuation of the Poles, but we had none to spare. Besides, we could not send cars to the Gustino line

where the majority of the Polish war prisoners were, since that line was already under fire. . . . Thus the Polish war prisoners remained in the Smolensk region. *Katyn Forest Massacre*, p. 229.

Extensive analysis and rebuttal of the Russian "investigation," not only by the London Polish government but later in testimony before the House Committee, removes what little plausibility the Russian contentions may have had for some contemporary observers. It was not customary for the Russians to employ officer prisoners as road-building labor. It was the invariable rule, on the other hand, for prisoners to be evacuated well in advance of the arrival of German troops. The failure of the Russians to account for the disappearance of the prisoners prior to the German announcement has never been explained, even by their own propaganda. The Russian contention that mail dated up to the summer of 1941 was found on the bodies remains unsupported by any witness from inside Poland who might have testified to contact with the prisoners after the spring of 1940. On the other hand, there is much evidence that the Polish prisoners were taken from their camps in groups of 200 to 300—except for a contingent of 400 whom the Russians hoped to convert to Communism and who thus survived.

American officer war prisoners, who were forced by the Nazis to observe the corpses at Katyn, also noted—as did other witnesses—that the Polish dead were clad in winter uniforms in an excellent state of repair, showing practically no wear. This was especially noteworthy with regard to their boots. The American prisoners stated that from their own personal experience as prisoners of war in a German camp they knew that clothing could not have remained in that condition if it had been worn for a year in a prisoner camp. The body of mutually reinforcing evidence supporting the Polish case on the Katyn massacre has become so impressive that it seems surprising, from today's vantage point, that contemporary U.S. and British official opinion generally credited the Russian case. It must be remembered, of course, that at that time Russia was bearing the heaviest burden of the war. For additional information on the Katyn massacre, cf. J. K. Zawodny, *Death in the Forest* (Notre Dame, Ind.: University of Notre Dame Press, 1962).

17. Mikolajczyk, p. 31.

18. George F. Kennan, *Russia and the West Under Lenin and Stalin* (Boston: Little, Brown, 1960), p. 360. Churchill appears to have thought the Polish declaration a mistake. When Sikorski placed the evidence of the Soviet murder of the officers before him, Churchill says he replied: "If they are dead nothing you can do will bring them back." (Churchill, *The Hinge of Fate,* p. 759.) According to Feis it is unclear whether Sikorski himself "was fully advised that the statement was to be issued,and, if he was, whether he favored or resisted it. . . . What is certainly clear is that the military elements in his government, and the leaders of the Polish Army, felt that Polish honor and human justice made it imperative to break silence on this question and to hold the Soviet Government up for judgment. Whoever within the Polish group had sponsored the statement, some of them soon began to regret it." Feis, p. 193n.

19. *Correspondence Between the Chairman of the Council of Ministers of the U.S.S.R. and the Presidents of the U.S.A. and the Prime Ministers of Great Britain During the Great Patriotic War of 1941-1945* (Moscow: Foreign Language Publishing House, 1957), I, 120-22 and II, 60-62. (This source will be referred to later as *Stalin Correspondence.*)

20. Hull *Memoirs,* II, 1266.

21. "We wanted to see normal diplomatic relations restored between Russia and Poland; and we wanted the Soviet Government to agree to broad principles of international cooperation after the war, centered around the creation of an organization to maintain the peace. But we did not intend to insist on a wartime settlement of specific questions such as the determination of the future boundary between Poland and Russia. Raising this question, at the insistence of the Polish Government or of anyone else, would have reopened the whole question of numerous boundaries of interest to Russia—a Pandora's box of infinite trouble—which we had successfully postponed for the time being by the strong stand we had emphatically taken when the British-Soviet agreement of May 26, 1942, was under negotiation." Hull *Memoirs,* II, 1273.

22. Mikolajcyzk, p. 45.

23. Jan Ciechanowski, *Defeat in Victory* (Garden City, N.Y.: Doubleday, 1947), pp. 215-16; Hull *Memoirs,* II, 1271-72.

24. Hull *Memoirs,* II, 1305.

25. Feis, pp. 208-209. Equally significant, though not in connection with Poland, was the difference between the originally proposed language of paragraph 2 and that which was finally accepted: "That those of them at war with the common enemy will act together in all matters relating to the surrender and disarmament of that enemy, *and to any occupation of enemy territory and territory of other states held by that enemy.*" The clause appearing in italics was deleted because of Molotov's objections.

26. Hull *Memoirs,* II, 1314-15.

27. Ibid., II, 1316. The full text of the eloquent parallel note to the British government is contained in Mikolajczyk, note 11, pp. 267 ff. The quoted passage about resistance to the Soviets was modified by the additional sentence: "In that case the Polish Government foresee the use of measures of self-defense wherever such measures are rendered indispensable by Soviet methods of terror and extermination of Polish citizens. . . ." The note went on to say: "The Polish Government have, moreover, reasons to fear that in present conditions the life and property of Polish citizens may be exposed to danger after the entry of Soviet troops into Poland and the imposing on the country of Soviet administration. In that case desperate reaction of the Polish community may be expected, following the violation of the principle adopted in Quebec, assuring to the United Nations their liberty and their own administration. . . . Polish airmen, sailors, and soldiers in carrying out the fight against the common enemy must be assured that their families will be restored to them and that they can expect to return to a free and independent homeland."

28. Churchill, *Closing the Ring,* p. 362.

29. Robert E. Sherwood, *Roosevelt and Hopkins* (New York: Harper, 1948), p. 796. Stalin's reply was to suggest that some propaganda work should be undertaken to bend their minds to accord with state policy. McNeill (p. 364) comments: "Stalin probably did not take Roosevelt's remarks seriously. It is likely that he regarded the President's appeal to Polish-American opinion as a curiously devious trick to justify a policy of opposition to the Soviet Union."

30. *Foreign Relations of the United States—Conferences of Cairo and Tehran* (Washington: Government Printing Office, 1961; here-

after cited as *Tehran Papers*), p. 594. Feis (p. 285) comments: "in telling Stalin that he found no fault with the general ideas of shifting Polish frontiers to the west, Roosevelt, according to his own later interpretation, did not mean to bestow his approval on any particular frontier line—specifically the Curzon Line. But Stalin and Molotov both understood him to be doing so." Cf. also Stalin's version of what Roosevelt said, as reported by Churchill in 1944 (*Tehran Papers*, p. 885) and Roosevelt's own recollection at Yalta (*Yalta Papers*, [see chap. 1, note 1], p. 667).

31. Sherwood, p. 786. McNeill (p. 357) comments on this episode: "What effect did Roosevelt's casual statement that American ground troops would not be available for police duty abroad have on Stalin's calculations? Stalin was a man who greatly respected military force. If America were in truth getting ready to withdraw militarily from Europe and Asia after the end of the war, obviously the only rival to his political influence would be Great Britain. . . . If Stalin thought in terms such as these, it is probable that Roosevelt's statement encouraged him to raise his sights higher and made the Russians more unbending than before in claiming territorial and other concessions for themselves in Eastern Europe."

32. Mikolajczyk, note 13, pp. 270 ff.

33. Ibid., pp. 51-52. "I cannot make such an announcement, Mr. Prime Minister," Mikolajczyk reports himself as having answered. "Poland cannot emerge from this war diminished. You are asking for an intolerable concession. . . . Let me tell you that this will be a test case. It will compromise an Allied nation grossly and unjustly, and it will not bring peace to Europe. Don't you see, Mr. Prime Minister, that the Soviet Union's aim is not only to take the eastern half of our country but to take all of Poland—all of Europe? We have tried so diligently to keep the unity of the Allies, to cooperate. But do you realize that since the Red Army entered Poland it has been disarming and arresting the very members of the Polish underground who helped the Russians capture each point?" To which, the Polish premier reports, Churchill replied with a shrug. "That's more of a reason why you should now quickly agree to the Curzon Line."

It deserves to be noted that Mikolajczyk put the Polish case usually in terms of the diminution of territory he was asked to accept, rather than in terms of population. This was probably because, according to the Polish 1931 census, the last one before the war, the population to the east of the Curzon Line was predominantly Ukrainian and Byelorussian. Of a total population of 10.6 million living in that area, 5.7 million had given Russian languages as their mother tongues. Some 0.9 million had indicated Yiddish, and most of these had presumably been killed by the Germans by the end of the war. Competent analysts believe that the figures of Ukrainians may have been understated in the census, since Poland had launched a policy of forced pacification against the Ukrainian nationalists in 1930. Cf. U. S. Department of Commerce, Bureau of the Census, *The Population of Poland* (Washington: Government Printing Office, 1954), pp. 74-79 and p. 149.

To say that the population to the east of the Curzon Line was predominantly Ukrainian and Byelorussian does not, of course, mean that that population desired to belong to the U. S. S. R., notwithstanding the "plebiscite" held in that area by the Russians in 1939. According to the census figures, the area in any event also contained a sizable minority of some 3.9 million Poles. Churchill in his conversations with Mikolajczyk always stated that Poles to the east of the Curzon Line would have the right to be repatriated to Poland proper. Cf. Mikolajczyk, p. 51.

34. "Hull asked the Ambassador to impress both the Soviet and Polish Governments with the wisdom of not doing anything that might affect full military cooperation, spoil the possibilities of international cooperation after the war, or affect adversely the President's prospects for election. But judgment as well as expediency influenced the American treatment of the situation. Roosevelt thought, and Harriman's and Winant's reports gave ground for the belief, that the Soviet Government was not without cause in its refusal to deal with the Polish Government until it ejected certain of its members. Some of its inner group were, in truth, making no secret of their hatred and complete mistrust of the Soviet Union. They were saying that the only real hope for Poland lay in war between the West and the Soviet Union." Feis, p. 296.

35. Ibid., p. 297. General Anders, who was in command of the Second Polish Corps, which was in the center of the hardest fighting

in Italy, sent a message on February 25, 1944 saying that "all soldiers of the Polish Army in the east will refuse to consider the possibility of abandoning any scrap of Polish territory to the Bolsheviks."

36. Mikolajczyk, p. 56; Ciechanowski, pp. 308 and 317.

37. Hull *Memoirs*, II, 1441-42.

38. *Stalin Correspondence*, I, 241-42.

39. "The Polish Army now entering Polish territory, trained in the USSR, is now joined to the People's Army to form the corps of the Polish armed forces, the armed arm of our nation in its struggle for independence. Its ranks will be joined tomorrow by the sons of Warsaw. . . . It is . . . a hundred times more necessary than ever to remember that in the flood of Hitlerite destruction all is lost that is not saved by active effort and that by direct active struggle in the streets of Warsaw, in its houses, factories, and stores we not only hasten the moment of final liberation but also save the nation's property and the lives of our brethren. Poles, the time of liberation is at hand! Poles, to arms! There is not a moment to lose!" Radio Kosciuszko, Moscow, in Polish, 8:15 p.m., July 29, 1944.

40. Churchill, *Triumph and Tragedy*, pp. 133-34.

41. Ibid., p. 141. Hull, in another context, addressed himself to the same hypothesis: "In connection with the Polish-Russian dispute then and later on, and in connection with other questions between us and Russia, a suggestion was advanced from time to time that all we had to do to bring about a settlement was to threaten that we would cut off the Lend-Lease assistance we were sending her. Neither the President nor I seriously entertained this suggestion for a moment. Russia, Britain, and the United States were in the same boat, which would float or sink depending on their abilities in jointly fighting the common enemy. Our Lend-Lease supplies to Russia were helping to pin down or eliminate enemy armed forces on the Eastern Front which otherwise we would have had to fight on the Western Front.

"The very making of such a threat would have engendered bad feeling between Moscow on the one hand and London and Washington on the other. Russia could always argue, moreover, as we ourselves had done, that the sending of aid to her was in our own best interests. If we made the threat and Russia refused to accede to our demands, we would then have faced a dilemma. Would we cut off military aid and thereby hurt ourselves militarily? Or would we continue it, thereby proving that our threat had been an empty one? And if we did cut it off, and let Moscow go its own way, could we then have the slightest hope of reaching a general postwar agreement with the Soviet Government?

"On the other hand, if Stalin bowed to such a threat—and we had not the slightest assurance he would do so—what valid hope could we cherish that an agreement negotiated under a virtual ultimatum would be carried out when the Axis Powers were defeated and Russia no longer needed our military help?" Hull *Memoirs*, II, 1272-73.

42. McNeill, pp. 432-33. The passage continues: "Indeed, the tragedy moved with the inevitability of Greek drama. Poland's fall, like that of Oedipus, came as a result of the defects of Polish virtues. Courage, pride, stubbornness, and impetuosity became folly and recklessness, and brought dire catastrophe. Catastrophe it was, for Russia as much as for Poland, and for the Western Powers as much as for Russia. The failure of Allied policy to achieve a peaceable settlement of the Polish problem in the first seven months of 1944 may well be considered the turning-point in the history of the Grand Alliance. Although a semblance of harmony was reestablished at Yalta in February, 1945, that harmony was never translated from words into deeds. Despite all later efforts to mend the breach between East and West, the bad blood created in Poland in 1944 proved the beginning of the end. . . ."

43. Mikolajczyk (pp. 97-98) poignantly narrates his dialogue with Churchill as follows: " 'How near we got at the beginning of the year!' he said, stalking around the room. 'If you had come to an agreement with the Russians at that time, you would not have today those Lublin people. They are going to be a frightful nuisance. They will build up a rival government and gradually take over authority in Poland.'

"I reminded him again of the Atlantic Charter and other pacts that directly or indirectly pledged sovereign rights to Poland.

" 'I shall tell Parliament that I have agreed with Stalin', Churchill declared flatly. 'Our relations with Russia are much better than they have ever been. I mean to keep them that way'.

"He added, 'I talked to your General Anders the other day, and he seems to entertain the hope that after the defeat of the Germans the Allies will then beat Russia. This is crazy! You cannot defeat the Russians! I beg of you to settle upon the Curzon Line as a frontier. Suppose you do lose the support of some of the Poles? Think what you will gain in return. You will have a country. . . .'

"I shook my head, and it infuriated him that I refused his compromise.

" 'Then I wash my hands of this', he stormed. 'We are not going to wreck the peace of Europe. In your obstinacy you do not see what is at stake. It is not in friendship that we shall part. We shall tell the world how unreasonable you are. You wish to start a war in which twenty-five million lives will be lost!'

" 'You settled our fate at Teheran', I said.

" 'Poland was *saved* at Teheran,' he shouted.

" 'I am not a person whose patriotism is diluted to the point where I would give away half my country', I answered."

According to Ciechanowski (p. 335), when Churchill was asked during the same conversation whether he would accept the cession of British territory if Britain found herself in such a situation, the British leader is supposed to have replied: "I certainly would, and be blessed by future generations. There is no other alternative. Poland is threatened with virtual extinction. . . ."

44. Churchill, *Triumph and Tragedy,* p. 240. One peculiar feature of Mikolajczyk's last conference with Stalin on that occasion was the Soviet leader's answer when the Polish premier bluntly asked him whether he intended to make Poland a Communist state after the war. Stalin is supposed to have replied, "No, absolutely not. Communism does not fit the Poles. They are too individualistic. Poland's future economy should be based on private enterprise. Poland will be a capitalistic state." Mikolajczyk, p. 100.

45. Ciechanowski, p. 347.

46. Ibid., pp. 341-42. On the idea that the world organization would solve the problems left unsolved during the war, George Kennan had commented earlier in a memorandum sent to the State Department from Moscow: "An international organization for the preservation of peace and security cannot take the place of a well-conceived and realistic foreign policy . . . and we are being . . . negli-

gent of the interests of our people if we allow plans for an international organization to be an excuse for failing to occupy ourselves seriously and minutely with the sheer power relationships of the European peoples." (Feis, p. 436).

47. *Stalin Correspondence*, II, 175.

48. Chester Wilmot, *The Struggle for Europe* (London: Collins, 1952), p. 584.

49. Royal Institute of International Affairs, *The Realignment of Europe*, edited by Arnold Toynbee (London: Oxford University Press, 1955), p. 190.

4

Mostly Poland:
Yalta and the Aftermath

At the time of the Yalta Conference, the Red Army was in possession of almost all prewar Poland. In a series of gigantic offensives in January 1945, it had cut across Poland and into Germany all the way to the Oder River and had spearheads only forty miles from Berlin. The Russians had advanced in the north to Danzig and cut off twenty-five German divisions in East Prussia. They were penetrating into Upper Silesia, the only German industrial area untouched by Allied bombing attacks; and in the south, they had advanced from Hungary to within eighty miles of Vienna. Meanwhile, in the west, the Allies had only just regained the line they had been holding six weeks before when the Rundstedt offensive had begun. Except for the Roer River sector, the fortified Siegfried Line was still intact; the Rhine had yet to be forced; and, as Wilmot reports, there was doubt in General Eisenhower's headquarters that a large-scale crossing of the lower Rhine could be carried out soon.[1]

Mostly Poland: Yalta and the Aftermath

This situation was, in large part, the result of Hitler's gamble in the Ardennes, for which he had committed the entire German strategic reserve. Hitler's purpose had been primarily political. By demonstrating to the Western Allies that victory was not certain, he still hoped to persuade them to make a separate peace. He followed with the closest attention every evidence of inter-Allied disagreements. He had exclaimed in December to the assembled generals that "if we can now deliver a few more heavy blows, then at any moment this artificially-bolstered common front may collapse with a gigantic clap of thunder."[2] After the disaster of the Russian offensive had struck him in January, he felt that at any moment a Western offer might come to him to prevent the Russians from advancing further toward the Atlantic.[3] His only hope now was a falling out among his enemies. The purpose of Roosevelt, Churchill, and Stalin was to demonstrate that such a falling out was not to be expected.

The Yalta Conference dealt with many subjects. With regard to the defeat of Germany, it resulted in an agreement to concert the final offensives from East and West. This was clearly in the mutual interest. The Western Allies considered that the crossing of the Rhine would expose their forces to the greatest danger, and they wanted assurances that no German troops could be drawn from the Eastern Front at that critical time. The Russians, on the other hand, were fearful that unless the Americans and British pressed their attacks in the West (and especially in Italy, where operations had quieted down), the Nazis might draw troops from those fronts and throw them to the East.[4] With respect to the Far East, agreement was reached on Russian entry into the war, and the Western leaders paid for this by giving Stalin assurances that Russia would obtain the territories and rights it had enjoyed before it was defeated by the Japanese in 1904, plus the Kurile Islands. The question of Ger-

77

man reparations was extensively discussed and seemed agreed in principle. With regard to the United Nations organization, the West obtained a major concession when Stalin gave up his insistence that disputes involving one of the great powers should not be discussed without its agreement. There was also agreement that only countries that declared war against Germany by March 1 should be admitted to initial United Nations membership. Here it must be noted, since Stalin made a point of it during his second conversation with Hopkins in May (see Chapter 2), that it was understood that Argentina, which had collaborated with the Axis throughout the war, would not be among the initial members of the new world organization.[5]

But by far the greatest amount of time spent by the Conference was on the subject of Poland. In the words of one historian, "the Polish question was a disheveled presence in every conference hour. It was discussed in the private talks which Churchill, Stalin, and Roosevelt had with one another; in the group meetings of the Foreign Ministers; and at all but one of the plenary sessions. It became the testing ground between the West and Communist Russia—between two conceptions of security."[6] The questions were still what would be the boundaries of the future Poland, and how the country was to be governed. To both of these questions, the conference in the end provided ambiguous answers.

The territorial question had meanwhile become further complicated by propaganda claims of the Polish Provisional Government in Warsaw to the effect that the Polish borders in the West should extend not only to the Oder but in its southern part along the Western Neisse river to the Czech border near Goerlitz, adding another sizable chunk of German territory over and above what Churchill thought he had agreed to at Tehran. As for the eastern boundary, Roosevelt pleaded rather than argued.

He referred once more to the six or seven million Poles in the United States and said, "It would make it easier for me at home if the Soviet Government could give something to Poland. I raised the question of giving them Lwow at Tehran. It has now been suggested that the oil lands in the southwest of Lwow might be given them. I am not making a definite statement but I hope that Marshal Stalin can make a gesture in this direction."[7] Churchill said that he stood by his agreement to the Curzon Line, but if Russia were to make a magnanimous concession, the British would heartily acclaim such action.

Stalin responded heatedly and at great length and with the arguments with which we are familiar since Chapter 2 of this study. Molotov followed up this statement with a draft which spoke of digressions from the Curzon Line in some regions "of 5 to 8 kilometers in favor of Poland." Churchill argued against extending the Polish border too far into German territory ("It would be a pity to stuff the Polish goose so full of German food that it got indigestion"). Roosevelt now circulated a written statement that the American government would not object if the Polish eastern frontier were set at the Curzon Line with small changes in Poland's favor as suggested by Molotov, but with regard to the western frontier he saw little justification for extending it up to the Western Neisse River.

The eastern border of Poland was thus settled. At the end of the Conference, since the western border was still not agreed, it was decided that the communique would record agreement among the three heads of government on the Curzon Line with digressions of 5 to 8 kilometers in favor of Poland, while stating that delimitation of the western frontier of Poland would be the subject of discussion with a new Polish government and "should thereafter await the Peace Conference." (As it turned out, the Russians turned over to Poland all the territory up to the Western Neisse, and the Poles soon set about expelling the entire German population, i.e., about three million more than Roosevelt and Churchill had been willing to see expelled. In the east, the frontier remained as already agreed in July 1944 between Russia and its chosen Polish instrument, the Lublin Committee.)

With regard to the future Polish government, both Roosevelt and Churchill recognized that some kind of fusion between the London and Lublin groups would have to take place. The question, although it was never clearly stated, was who would be in the majority. The three leaders agreed on the necessity for early elections, so that their discussion concerned—or seemed to concern—only the composition of a new provisional government (a "Provisional Government of National Unity") that would operate until the time when elections could be held, which according to Stalin might be "in about one month." Churchill put forward the names of three candidates for inclusion in the new Provisional Government—Mikolajczyk, Grabski, and Romer—but Stalin declared that it would be unthinkable for the Big Three themselves to put together a new Polish government. After all, there existed a Provisional Government (the "Lublin" government) in Warsaw, and the point of departure for any solution would have to be a consultation with the leaders of that pro-Soviet group. As it turned out, however, Stalin was unable to reach the leaders of the Lublin group by telephone; so it was agreed that the necessary consultations with the various Polish leaders would take place not in Yalta, but later in Moscow. The discussion thus turned to the terms of reference under which those consultations were to be held.

The matter of wording now becomes important, for the charges and countercharges of bad faith in implementing the Yalta decision regarding Poland turn on the precise phrasing of the agreement and the manner in which it was arrived at. The British proposal of February 8 read: "Having regard to the recent liberation of western Poland by the Soviet armies it was deemed desirable to facilitate *the establishment of a fully representative provisional Polish Government* based upon all the democratic and anti-Fascist forces in Poland and including democratic leaders from the Poles abroad. That Government should be so constituted as to command recognition by the three Allied Governments." (The italics are supplied here to emphasize the most important differences between the principal drafts.) The British draft went on to state that the provisional government should then "as soon as possible hold free and unfettered elections on the basis of universal suffrage and secret ballot, in which all democratic parties should have the right to participate and to promote candidatures, in order to ensure the establishment of a Government truly representative of the will of the Polish people."[8]

The Russians did not like the British draft. Molotov stated that the discussions should deal *not with creation of an entirely new government but with enlargement of the existing Provisional Government* through the addition of other democratic elements from within Poland and abroad. He claimed that the Lublin, or Warsaw, government enjoyed great prestige and popularity and said the Poles would never agree to any solution which would greatly change that Provisional Government. He said, "if we wish to achieve a practical result it should be done on the basis of the enlargement of the present government, but how many and who they should be is the subject we should talk about." He gave an indication of the Russian thinking by suggesting that in the first instance, three members of the Provisional Government and two Poles suggested by President Roosevelt should be invited to consult with a three-power commission to be established in Moscow. He argued that after all the whole matter concerned only an interim government pending the holding of free elections. Churchill immediately argued against this position and in favor of creating a completely new government. An impasse had been reached.[9]

Next day the American delegation came forward with what it thought was a compromise between the Russian and British positions. The relevant passage of the American draft read: "That *the present Polish Provisional Government be reorganized* into a fully representative government based on all democratic forces in Poland and including democratic leaders from Poland abroad, to be termed 'The Provisional Government of National Unity'." The U. S. draft had wording similar to the British draft with respect to the holding of free elections, and ended: "When a 'Provisional Government of National Unity' is satisfactorily formed, the three Governments will then proceed to accord it recognition. The Ambassadors of the three powers in Warsaw following such recognition would be charged with the responsibility of observing and reporting to their respective Governments on the carrying out of the pledge in regard to free and unfettered elections."[10]

The British did not like the American draft. As Eden stated in the Foreign Ministers' meeting on February 9, according to the Page minutes: "As regards the Lublin Provisional Government, it was possible that he might be quite wrong but he thought it was a fact that hardly anyone in Great Britain believed that the Lublin Government was representative of Poland. He should have thought that that view was widely held in the rest of Europe and in the United States of America. It was for that reason that the document which he had put forward the previous day *had avoided all mention of adding to the Lublin Government and had stressed that a new start was nec-*

essary."[11] This statement focused with almost embarrassing clarity on the magnitude of the apparent concession contained in the American draft—although both the British and American governments would later strenuously deny that such a concession had been made.

The Russian proposal made by Molotov at the plenary meeting on February 9 involved only some editing of the first sentence of the American draft, which he wanted reworded as follows: "The present Provisional Government of Poland shall be reorganized on a wider democratic basis with the inclusion of democratic leaders from Poland itself and from those living abroad, and in this connection this government would be called the National Provisional Government of Poland." The Soviet foreign minister also said, however, that the last sentence dealing with the responsibilities of the ambassadors of the three governments in Warsaw to observe and report on the carrying out of the free elections should be eliminated since he "felt certain that it would be offensive to the Poles and would needlessly complicate the discussion."[12]

According to the Bohlen minutes of that meeting, President Roosevelt remarked that after studying Molotov's amendment to the first sentence he thought

we were now very near agreement and it was only a matter of drafting. He said that for those governments which still recognized the London Government the use of the words "Provisional Government" (to describe the Lublin group) was somewhat difficult, and he felt that the first words of Mr. Molotov's amendment might read "The Government now operating in Poland." He said he felt it was very important for him in the U. S. that there be some gesture made for the six million Poles there indicating that the U. S. was in some way involved with the question of freedom of elections, and he therefore felt that the last sentence con-

83

cerning the reports of the Ambassadors was important. He repeated that he felt, however, that it was only a matter of words and details and the three Foreign Ministers might meet tonight and discuss it.[13]

Churchill bore in more heavily on the question of free elections, for which some kind of international observation was a precondition. He referred to the absence of diplomatic reporting from inside Poland and to disquieting reports about the intention of the Lublin government to try as traitors all members of the Polish Home Army. Archly, he observed that "in Egypt whatever government conducts the elections, wins." He recognized the force of Stalin's argument that as long as the Red Army's lines stretched across Poland, the Russians had legitimate security concerns.[14] Both Churchill and Roosevelt argued that they were concerned not only with principle but also with practical politics.[15] Finally, however, Secretary of State Stettinius on Roosevelt's instruction agreed to drop the clause about the ambassadors "observing and reporting" to which Molotov had objected, although Eden wished it to be understood that he did not agree with the American proposal to drop that clause.[16]

In the end, the Declaration on Poland agreed at the Conference was as indicated on page ix of this study, with a middle paragraph about the mechanics of implementation to the effect that "Mr. Molotov, Mr. Harriman and Sir A. Clark Kerr are authorised as a Commission to consult in the first instance in Moscow with members of the present Provisional Government and with other Polish democratic leaders from within Poland and from abroad, with a view to the reorganisation of the present Government along the above lines." (It will be noted that the Declaration thus speaks not once, but twice, of *"reorganizing* the *present* government.") With respect to the right of ambassadors to observe the carrying out of the agreement, there only remained the innocuous sentence: "When a Polish Provisional Government of National Unity has been properly formed in conformity with the above, the Government of the USSR, which now maintains diplomatic relations with the present Provisional Government of Poland, and the Government of the United Kingdom and the Government of the USA will establish diplomatic relations with the new Polish Provisional Government of National Unity, and will exchange Ambassadors by whose reports the respective Governments will be kept informed about the situation in Poland." As Churchill dryly remarked after reporting his last conversation on the subject with Stalin, "This was the best I could get."[17]

A factor which helped to sweeten the Polish pill for Roosevelt and Churchill was Stalin's acceptance of a Declaration on Liberated Europe. That document had been drawn up in the State Department and was introduced rather late in the Conference. The debate on it was perfunctory, and it was agreed after Molotov watered down the operative clause.[18] (The key passages will be found on page viii above.) In the mind of its drafters, the Declaration was intended to establish the principle of joint tripartite responsibility in eastern Europe, and it was to counteract the idea of spheres of influence, which, as we shall see, had been pursued by both Churchill and Stalin (cf. Chapter 5). Every unilateral act by the Russians in eastern Europe could henceforth be branded as a violation of the Declaration on Liberated Europe. It is worth noting, however, that the operative clause of the Declaration required the Russians only to "consult," and even this could apparently take place only when all three of the Allies judged it necessary.

The Yalta decisions were hailed in Britain and the United States as heartening evidence of Allied harmony not only in bringing the war to a successful conclusion but also in building a better world. There were some misgivings about Poland, but major criticisms of Yalta occurred only later, when it became known that there had been secret agreements with respect to China and to the effect that Russia should have three seats in the United Nations. In the House of Commons, Churchill defended the agreement on Poland as the best that could be obtained, and it was in this spirit that it was approved.[19] Meanwhile, Nazi propaganda claimed that Yalta represented a sellout to Stalin, that it confirmed Russian overlordship in east and southeast Europe and the major part of Germany, and that an "iron curtain" would descend on the middle of Europe if Germany were to lay down its arms.[20]

The scene now shifted to Moscow, where, under the Declaration on Poland, Molotov and the American and British ambassadors were to consult with members of the existing Provisional Government and with other Polish democratic leaders from within Poland and abroad, "with a view to the reorganization of the present Government" on a broader democratic basis. And of course they immediately disagreed on the interpretation of the Yalta agreement. Molotov insisted that only Polish leaders who supported the Yalta decisions should be consulted about reorganizing the Provisional Government. This excluded even Mikolajczyk, who had publicly protested against the decision on Poland's eastern boundary, and in effect limited the field to Communists and their sympathizers. Moreover, the Russians made it clear that any reorganization of the pro-Communist government in Warsaw would in their view consist of merely adding a small minority of non-Communist Poles. It was obvious that if this were done, the chances of non-Communist leaders to rally their followers in preparation for an election would be very slim indeed. A further downgrading of the recent Allied agreements seemed to be implied when the Russians announced that Foreign Minister Molotov would not attend the San Francisco Conference where the United Nations was to be born.

In the dispute over the implementation of the Yalta agreements there now supervened an ugly episode when Stalin believed, or professed to believe, that the Western Allies were double-crossing him by negotiating a separate armistice with the Germans in Italy. Local German commanders there had put out feelers for an armistice, and this was immediately reported by the West to their Russian ally. While preliminary contacts were taking place at Berne, the Russian government complained that "negotiations" were taking place without Russian representation. When it was explained to Molotov that there were no negotiations and that, were they to take place, the Russians would be fully associated with them, the Foreign Minister refused to accept this and stated that "in this instance the Soviet Government sees not a misunderstanding, but something worse."[21]

President Roosevelt in a personal message to Stalin explained that no negotiations had taken place in Switzerland, but Stalin replied complaining that "the Germans have already taken advantage of the talks with the Allied Command to move three divisions from Northern Italy to the Soviet front" and he insisted that Roosevelt was wrong and that negotiations were actually taking place with the Germans in Berne.[22] Roosevelt categorically denied this, but Stalin came back claiming he had better information. (There was a parallel correspondence with Churchill.) "I realize," Stalin wrote, "that there are certain ad vantages resulting to the Anglo-American troops from the separate negotiations in Berne or in some other place, seeing that the Anglo-American troops are enabled to advance into the heart of Germany almost without resistance; but why conceal this from the Russians. . . ?" Stalin suspected that the reason was that the Western Allies had "promised, in exchange, to ease the armistice terms for the Germans." He even claimed that an agreement along such lines was about to be concluded and might already be in effect.[23]

"I have received with astonishment your message of April 3" (containing the above allegations), Roosevelt replied immediately. He reviewed what had actually happened at Berne and added: "For the advantage of our common war effort against Germany, which today gives excellent promise of an early success in a disintegration of the German Armies, I must continue to assume that you have the same high confidence in my truthfulness and reliability that I have always had in yours." But Stalin would not back down. He still insisted that he was better informed than Roosevelt and argued: "It is hard to agree that the absence of German resistance on the Western Front is due solely to the fact that they have been beaten. The Germans . . . are fighting desperately against the Russians for Zemlenice, an obscure station in Czechoslovakia, which they need just as much as a dead man needs a poultice, but they surrender without any resistance such important towns in the heart of Germany as Osnabrueck, Mannheim and Kassel. You will admit that this behavior on the part of the Germans is more than strange and unaccountable."[24] The episode came to an end because the Germans in Italy never produced actual negotiators. But it marked a low point in the dealings between Stalin on the one hand and Roosevelt and Churchill on the other, in which there were accusations of treachery and expressions of bitter resentment at the very time when victory over Germany was being achieved.

It was in this atomsphere that Roosevelt and Stalin exchanged personal messages about Russia's failure to live up to the Yalta agreement on Poland. Roosevelt's message, sent less than two weeks before his death, also pleaded that the United Nations be not depreciated by having Russia represented by someone other than Molotov. The message ended:

> I wish I could convey to you how important it is for the successful development of our program of international collaboration that this Polish question be settled fairly and speedily. If this is not done all of the difficulties and dangers to Allied unity which we had so much in mind in reaching our decisions at the Crimea will face us in an even more acute form. You are, I am sure, aware that genuine popular support in the U. S. is required to carry out any government policy, foreign or domestic. The American people make up their own mind and no government action can change it. I mention this fact because the last sentence of your message about Mr. Molotov's attendance at San Francisco made me wonder whether you give full weight to this factor.[25]

As to the substance of the disagreement on Poland, Roosevelt addressed himself in two key paragraphs to the question of whether the new Provisional Government was to represent a completely fresh start, and to the question how its members were to be picked. On the first subject, he wrote:

> In the discussions that have taken place so far your Government appears to take the position that the new Polish Provisional Government of National Unity which we agreed should be formed should be little more than a continuation of the present Warsaw Government. I cannot reconcile this either with our agreement or our discussions. While it is true that the Lublin Government is to be reorganized and its members play a prominent role, it is to be done in such a fashion as to bring into being a new government. This point is clearly brought out in several

places in the text of the Agreement. I must make it quite plain to you that any such solution which would result in a thinly disguised continuance of the present Warsaw regime would be unacceptable and would cause the people of the U. S. to regard the Yalta agreements as having failed.

On the matter of picking members for the new government, Roosevelt wrote:

> It is equally apparent that for the same reason the Warsaw Government cannot under the Agreement claim the right to select or reject what Poles are to be brought to Moscow by the Commission for consultation. Can we not agree that it is up to the Commission to select the Polish leaders to come to Moscow to consult in the first instance and invitations be sent out accordingly. . . . We have not and would not bar or veto any candidate for consultation which Mr. Molotov might propose, being confident that he would not suggest any Poles who would be inimical to the intent of the Crimea decision. I feel it is not too much to ask that my Ambassador be accorded the same confidence and that any candidate for consultation presented by any one of the Commission be accepted by the others in good faith. It is obvious to me that if the right of the Commission to select these Poles is limited or shared with the Warsaw Government the very foundation on which our agreement rests would be destroyed.[26]

Roosevelt sent this message at the urging of Churchill, who sent a stronger parallel message to Stalin.[27] There is evidence, not all of it published as yet, that the American President at least at one time had doubts about this controversy over Poland and that he perhaps realized that the principal point had already been given away at Yalta. In a message to Churchill which perhaps predated this exchange with Stalin, he warned that "If we attempt to evade the fact that we placed, as clearly shown by the [Yalta] agreement, somewhat more emphasis on the Lublin Poles than on the other two groups from which the new Government is to be drawn, we expose ourselves to the charge that we are attempting to go back on the Crimea decision."[28] However, Roosevelt did feel that the Western Allies had every right to resist the Lublin group's claim to a veto over what Poles were to be consulted. (As we shall see, President Truman was not sensitive to this differentiated emphasis as between the two contentious questions about the Yalta agreement on Poland.)

Stalin's reply, five days before Roosevelt's death, did nothing to narrow the difference. He claimed that the reason for the impasse over Poland was "that the U. S. and British Ambassadors in Moscow . . . have departed from the instructions of the Crimea Conference." With regard to the nature of the government that was to be formed, he wrote:

> At the Crimea Conference the three of us regarded the Polish Provisional Government as the government now functioning in Poland and subject to reconstruction, as the government that should be the core of the new Government of National Unity. The U. S. and British Ambassadors, however . . . ignore the Polish Provisional Government . . . and at best place individuals in Poland and London on a par with the Provisional Government. Furthermore, they hold that reconstruction of the Provisional Government should be understood in terms of its abolition and the establishment of an entirely new government. . . . Obviously, this thesis cannot but be strongly resented by the Polish Provisional Government. As regards the Soviet Union, it certainly cannot accept a thesis that is tantamount to direct violation of the Crimea Conference decisions.

On the matter of invitations to Poles to appear before the Commission for consultations on the formation of a new government, Stalin took the position that they must be issued not by individual members of the Commission but "by the Commission as a whole, as a body"—in other words, that Russia should have a veto. He went on to say:

> The Soviet Government proceeds from the assumption that, by virtue of the Crimea decisions, those invited for consultation should be in the first instance Polish leaders who recognize the decisions of the Crimea Conference, including the one of the Curzon Line, and, secondly, who actually want friendly relations between Poland and the Soviet Union. The Soviet Government insists on this because the blood of Soviet soldiers, so freely shed in liberating Poland, and the fact that in the past thirty years the territory of Poland has twice been used by an enemy for invading Russia, oblige the Soviet Government to ensure friendly relations between the Soviet Union and Poland.[29]

As an indication of the proportions between cabinet members of the existing Warsaw government and outsiders which Stalin considered appropriate, he suggested using Yugoslavia as a model. There Tito had nominated twenty-one cabinet members and Subasic, the exile leader, had nominated only six. This message of Stalin, his last to Roosevelt, was dated April 7.

Let us pause here to throw a glance at the newspaper headlines of that first week of April 1945: On April 1, the U. S. Tenth Army landed in Okinawa. . . . On April 2, it was announced that the Allied 21st Army Group had pushed to 100 miles north and northeast of the Rhine. . . . On April 3, General Eisenhower made it known that the German Army Group B and part of Army Group H were cut off by Allied encirclement of the Ruhr. . . . On April 4, the French First Army entered Karlsruhe, while the Russians captured Bratislava. . . . On April 5, Molotov informed the Japanese ambassador that the Soviet government desired to denounce the Russian-Japanese Neutrality Act. . . . On April 6, the U. S. fleet off Okinawa was attacked by a strong force of Japanese suicide aircraft. On the same day, the Polish government in London issued a statement reporting that fifteen members of its erstwhile underground, including the deputy prime minister and the last commander of the Polish Home Army, had been invited to meetings with Soviet General Ivanov on March 27 and 28, for which safe conduct was guaranteed, but since those dates no news of any of those Poles had been received. . . . Also on April 6, Secretary Stettinius declared that the United States was doing everything in its power to promote the establishment of a representative Polish government as promised at the Crimea Conference, in time to be represented at the San Francisco Conference. . . . On April 7, the Russians announced that they had reached Vienna.

When President Truman was briefed by the State Department on April 13, the day after Roosevelt's death, the rundown of important pending foreign policy problems included these summary passages: "Since the Yalta Conference the Soviet Government has taken a firm and uncompromising position on nearly every major question that has arisen in our relations. The more important of these are the Polish question, the application of the Crimea agreement on liberated areas, the agreement on the exchange of liberated prisoners of war and civilians, and the San Francisco Conference." Under the heading of Poland, the briefing paper said:

> The present situation relating to Poland is highly unsatisfactory with the Soviet authorities consistently sabotaging Ambassador Harriman's efforts in the Moscow Commission to hasten the implementation of the decisions at the Crimea Conference. Direct appeals to Marshal Stalin have not yet produced any worth-while results. The Soviet Government likewise seeks to complicate the problem by initiating and supporting claims of the Warsaw Provisional Polish Gov-

93

ernment to represent and speak for Poland in international matters such as the San Francisco Conference. . . . Because of its effects on our relations with the Soviet Union and other United Nations and upon public opinion in this country, the question of the future status of Poland and its government remains one of our most complex and urgent problems both in the international and the domestic field.[30]

One positive development in this bleak picture occurred when Ambassador Harriman conferred with Stalin immediately after the news of Roosevelt's death had been conveyed to him. Stalin voiced his deep sorrow and expressed a willingness to work with the new President as he had with Roosevelt. Harriman, seizing this opening, suggested that the most effective method of assuring the United States and the world of the Soviet desire to continue collaboration would be for Molotov to go to the United States, first to see President Truman, and second to attend the conference at San Francisco. Stalin replied that if such a request came to him from the new President, he would comply with it. And so Molotov came to Washington—but his visit there worsened rather than improved the situation.

Before Molotov arrived in Washington, the situation had become still more tense because of two developments: on April 21, despite protests by the British and U. S. governments, Russia had signed a treaty of mutual assistance with the Polish Provisional Government, thereby lending emphasis to its position that that government was to be merely "reorganized" with the addition of a few outsiders but without any possible change of its basic pro-Soviet policies. On the other hand, Churchill and Truman had sent another message to Stalin in which they had rejected the Russian position and suggested, as a "constructive suggestion," that there be invited to the consultations in Moscow three members of the Warsaw Provisional Government; three members of the London government; and two non-Communist figures from inside Poland—thus making a clear non-Communist majority. The two Western leaders had said that the Warsaw government would unquestionably play a "prominent" part in the "new" provisional government, but they could not admit that it should dominate that government. "The real issue between us," they had said, "is whether or not the Warsaw Government has the right to veto individual candidates for consultation. No such interpretation in our considered opinion can be found in the Crimea decision. . . ." Churchill and Truman had also firmly rejected the applicability of the Yugoslav pattern to Poland.[31]

The dispute became still hotter when President Truman received Molotov at the White House. Upon being briefed on the continued deadlock on the foreign minister level (Stettinius, Eden, and Molotov had met in Washington and got nowhere in their discussion), the new President decided, as he reports in his memoirs, that "it was now obvious that our agreements with the Soviet Union had so far been a one-way street and that this could not continue." He took counsel with Stettinius, Secretary of War Stimson, Navy Secretary Forrestal, Admiral King, General Marshall, Ambassador Harriman, and other advisers. The record of that consultation is exceedingly revealing of the differing viewpoints on what should or could be done.[32] Truman sided with those who counseled toughness, and in very blunt terms he told Molotov that the United States considered that Russia had gone back on the agreement reached at Yalta. He hinted broadly that Russia could give up any hope for American postwar assistance if it did not satisfy American public opinion. And he handed Molotov a note ("For Information of Marshal Stalin") which contained the key phrase: "The U. S. Government cannot be a party to any method of consultation with

95

Polish leaders which would not result in the establishment of a new Provisional Government of National Unity genuinely representative of the democratic elements of the Polish people."[33]

Molotov remonstrated. He said that in the past the Big Three governments had been able to work out their differences, but now it appeared that two of them were attempting to impose their will on the third. Truman interrupted to say that all the United States was asking was that the Soviet government carry out the Crimea decision on Poland. Molotov said Russia stood by the Crimea decision. "I replied sharply," Truman recalls, "that an agreement had been reached on Poland and that there was only one thing to do and that was for Marshal Stalin to carry out that agreement in accordance with his word." Molotov said Stalin had given his views in the message of April 7, and he could not understand why, if the three governments could reach an agreement on the question of the composition of the Yugoslav government, the same formula could not apply in the case of Poland. "Replying sharply again," Truman recalls, "I said that an agreement had been reached on Poland and that it only required to be carried out by the Soviet Government."

Molotov repeated that his government supported the Crimea decisions but that he could not agree that an "abrogation" of those decisions by others could be considered a violation by the Soviet government. He added that surely the Polish question, involving as it did a neighboring country, was of very great interest to the Soviet Union. "Since Molotov insisted on avoiding the main issue," Truman recalls, "I said what I had said before—that the U. S. Government was prepared to carry out loyally all the agreements reached at Yalta and asked only that the Soviet Government do the same. I expressed once more the desire of the U. S. for friendship with Russia, but I wanted it clearly understood that this could be only on a basis of the mutual observation of agreements and not on the basis of a one-way street. 'I have never been talked to like that in my life,' Molotov said. I told him, 'Carry out your agreements and you won't get talked to like that'."[34] And thus ended a singularly sterile interview.

The President's memorandum was handed to Molotov on April 23. On April 24 Stalin sent his reply to both the memorandum and the Churchill-Truman message. The reply said, among other things:

> [Your] messages indicate that you still regard the Polish Provisional Government, not as the core of a future Polish Government of National Unity, but merely as a group on a par with any other group of Poles. It would be hard to reconcile this concept of the position of the Provisional Government and this attitude towards it with the Crimea decision on Poland. At the Crimea Conference the three of us, including President Roosevelt, based ourselves on the assumption that the Polish Provisional Government, as the Government now functioning in Poland and enjoying the trust and support of the majority of the Polish people, should be the core, that is, the main part of a new, reconstructed Polish Government of National Unity. . . .
>
> Another circumstance that should be borne in mind [Stalin added] is that Poland borders on the Soviet Union, which cannot be said about Great Britain or the U. S. A. Poland is to the security of the Soviet Union what Belgium and Greece are to the security of Great Britain. . . . I do not know whether a genuinely representative Government has been established in Greece, or whether the Belgium Government is a genuinely democratic one. The Soviet Union was not consulted when those Governments were being formed, nor did it claim the right to interfere in those matters, because it realizes how important Belgium and Greece are to the security of Great Britain. . . . I cannot understand why in discussing Poland no attempt is made to consider the interests of the Soviet Union in terms of security as

97

well. One cannot but recognize as unusual a situation in which two Governments—those of the U. S. and Great Britain—reach agreement beforehand on Poland, a country in which the USSR is interested first of all and most of all, and place its representatives in an intolerable position, trying to dictate to it. I say that this situation cannot contribute to agreed settlement of the Polish problem. I am ready to accede to your request and to do all in my power to reach an agreed settlement. But you are asking too much. To put it plainly, you want me to renounce the interests of the security of the Soviet Union; but I cannot proceed against the interests of my country.[35]

The next scene of the drama was played at San Francisco, but it differed from the previous scenes in that it was played before the world public. Up to this point, all the correspondence between the heads of state had of course been secret and most of the other events since Yalta had found only muted and muffled reflection in the public press and had in any event been vastly overshadowed by the spectacular news about the final battles of the war. (On the day the San Francisco Conference opened, April 25, Russian and American troops, having fought their way through Germany from East and West, met on the Elbe River.) At the conference, the Polish issue almost immediately precipitated a violent public quarrel as Molotov demanded that the Provisional Government of Poland be invited to the Conference. Stettinius, seconded by Eden, took the position that until a "new and representative" Polish Provisional Government was created in conformity with the Yalta decision, an invitation to—and thus recognition of—the Lublin government "would be a sordid exhibition of bad faith."[36] Russia was overwhelmingly voted down. Next the admission of Argentina came up, and again Russia was overwhelmingly voted down, although Molotov on his part now cited a Yalta conference decision.[37]

98

Mostly Poland: Yalta and the Aftermath

At San Francisco, Stettinius, Eden, and Molotov also continued their negotiations on the formation of a new Polish government, but their deadlock continued. Meanwhile, Churchill had sent yet another message to Stalin, the longest he ever wrote to the Russian leader during their wartime correspondence. Churchill insisted that in the new government there should be "a proper balance and a proper distribution of important posts in the government; this result should be reached as we agreed at the Crimea by discussing the matter, with true representatives of all the different Polish elements which are not fundamentally anti-Russian." The British leader closed his message with these prophetic words:

> "There is not much comfort in looking into a future where you and the countries you dominate, plus the Communist parties in many other States, are all drawn up on one side, and those who rally to the English-speaking nations and their Associates or Dominions are on the other. It is quite obvious that their quarrel would tear the world to pieces and that all of us leading men on either side who had anything to do with that would be shamed before history. . . . I hope there is no word or phrase in this outpouring of my heart to you which unwittingly gives offence. If so, let me know. But do not, I beg of you, my friend Stalin, underrate the divergencies which are opening about matters which you may think are small to us but which are symbolic of the way the English-speaking democracies look at life.[38]

On May 3 Molotov revealed at San Francisco that Soviet authorities had indeed arrested sixteen leaders of the Polish underground and that they were charging them with preparing and carrying out subversive activities against the Red Army. Eden and Stettinius thereupon decided to break off the negotiation. On May 5 Stalin sent his reply to Churchill, of which excerpts will be given further below. On May 8 the war in

99

Europe officially ended with the German capitulation at Reims. (The Russians held off their victory announcement until May 9, when the ceremony had to be repeated in Berlin.) On the same day, President Truman signed the order terminating Lend-Lease (see Chapter 6). On May 9 Molotov left San Francisco for Moscow, leaving behind a deadlock not only on the Polish question but also on the question, vital to the very existence of the United Nations, whether a dispute involving one of the Great Powers could be discussed in the Security Council without its consent.[39]

As we are now approaching the end of this chapter, having brought the story almost to the time of the Hopkins-Stalin conversations, it may be helpful to summarize the situation of the two sides with respect to Poland. The issue was basically whether the Communists and their allies, or the essentially anti-Soviet conservatives in Poland, would have a majority in the new government. Historians may argue inconclusively whether the Western leaders had in effect yielded the substance of this point to the Soviets in Yalta—but it is a fact that Churchill and Truman did not think so. They pressed, as had Roosevelt, for a new Polish government genuinely responsive to the will of the people. To Stalin it was obvious that any such government would be hostile to Russia—and from what we have seen in Chapter 3, the majority of patriotic Poles had indeed good reason to be hostile. The Russian dictator came very close to admitting this in his reply to Churchill dated May 4.

> The United Nations are interested in constant and durable friendship between the USSR and Poland [he wrote]. Hence we cannot acquiesce in the attempts that are being made to involve in the forming of the future Polish Government people who, to quote you, "are not fundamentally

anti-Russian" or to bar from participation only those who, to quote you, are "extreme people unfriendly to Russia." Neither one nor the other can satisfy us. We insist, and shall continue to insist, that only people who have demonstrated by deeds their friendly attitude to the Soviet Union, who are willing honestly and sincerely to cooperate with the Soviet state, should be consulted on the formation of a future Polish Government.[40]

Clearly, if such qualification were to be accepted, there would be no democracy in Poland as the West understood it. And, as it turned out, that is what happened.

The Hopkins mission to Moscow (Chapter 2) resulted in a compromise under which there were to be invited to "consult" on the formation of a new Polish government: four leaders of the Lublin group; three Poles from London (but not from the government-in-exile); and five from Poland. However, one of the three Poles from London was a Lublin Pole, and "three or four" of the five invited from Poland were sympathetic to the Lublin group.[41] When the consultation finally did take place, seven of the twelve Poles invited to Moscow were Communists or pro-Communists, and when the new Provisional Polish Government of National Unity was formed, fourteen of its twenty-one cabinet seats, including the ministries most valuable for the internal control of the country, went to veterans of the Lublin Committee. With the Polish issue settled, Stalin immediately withdrew his objection to the voting formula in the United Nations, Allied administrative arrangements in Germany were regularized, agreement on Allied administration of Austria was reached in the European Advisory Commission (where it had been hung up for months), and the ground was prepared for the Potsdam Conference. Stalin even expressed gratitude for Lend-Lease.[42] But the dispute over Russian control of Poland was not over. Indeed, as we shall see in the next chapter, it broadened into a dispute over Russian control over most of eastern and southeastern Europe.

By the time of the Potsdam Conference in July 1945, the United States and Great Britain had recognized the new Communist-dominated Polish government, though stressing its obligation to "hold free and unfettered elections as soon as possible" in accordance with the Yalta decision (cf. page ix). Both Churchill and Truman pressed Stalin for public assurances that the Polish elections should also be freely observed by the world press, and Truman emphasized the importance of this issue as a factor in American domestic politics. "There are six million Poles in the United States," he said. "A free election in Poland reported to the United States by a free press would make it much easier to deal with these Polish people."[43] Stalin, after some argument, agreed to include in the Potsdam communiqué some words about the observation of free elections.[44] But although the Soviet premier had told Roosevelt at Yalta that elections could take place in Poland one month after the country's liberation,[45] it was actually only two years later, in January 1947, that elections were held—after the non-Communist parties in Poland had been thoroughly terrorized, their news censored, their meetings often banned, and some of their leaders jailed.[46]

NOTES

1. Chester Wilmot, *The Struggle for Europe* (London: Collins, 1952), p. 631.

2. Ibid., p. 578.

3. Ibid., p. 626. Hitler suggested that, if only the Russians would proclaim a National Government for Germany, the English would "really start to be scared." Then he went on, "I have given orders that a report be played into their hands to the effect that the Russians are organizing 200,000 of our men led by German officers and completely infected with Communism, who will come marching into Germany. . . . That will make them feel as if someone had stuck a needle into them." (*Fuehrer Conferences*, Fragment 24, January 27, 1945, quoted by Wilmot.)

4. Herbert Feis, *Churchill, Roosevelt, Stalin—The War They Waged and the Peace They Sought* (Princeton, N.J.: Princeton University Press, 1957), pp. 498-99; *Yalta Papers* (See chap. 1, note 1), pp. 597 and 646.

5. Argentina declared war on Germany only on March 27, 1945, after the Inter-American Conference at Chapultepec, Mexico City, had called upon it to do so. According to James F. Byrnes, *Speaking Frankly* (New York: Harper, 1947), p. 39, Roosevelt and Stalin agreed at Yalta that with respect to Argentina and Turkey, not only the date of the declaration of war but also their status as associated nations who had helped in the war effort should govern the invitation. In any event, the Argentine declaration of war was after the agreed cut-off date of March 1. (Cf. also *Yalta Papers*, p. 773.) At Chapultepec, however, Stettinius yielded to Latin American pressure and agreed to support Argentina's entry provided it fulfilled certain conditions. It was a moot point, up to the time of the San Francisco Conference, whether all those conditions had been fulfilled. President Truman, who was consulted just before the Conference, was strongly opposed to Argentine adherence to the United Nations Declaration. Later, however, the matter became embroiled with Russia's demand that Poland be invited to the Conference, and in the end Stettinius was given a free hand. Ruth B. Russell, *A History of the United Nations Charter* (Washington: Brookings Institution, 1958), pp. 632, 636-37.

Cordell Hull has said about this episode: "To Secretary Stettinius over the telephone I spoke as strongly as I could against admitting Argentina to the San Francisco Conference. I said that the American delegation had to regain the leadership in the Argentine question that the United States had lost at the Mexico City Conference. . . . I would have voted against the admission of Argentina to the United Nations had I been called upon to vote. I was suddenly informed, however, that our delegation had already voted unanimously to admit her. I also said to Stettinius that if the American delegation were not careful we should get Russia into such a state of mind that she might decide that the United Nations organization was not going to furnish adequate security to her in the future." Hull, although a member of the U.S. delegation, was at the time in a hospital in Washington. *The Memoirs of Cordell Hull* (New York: Macmillan, 1948), II, 1722.

6. Feis, p. 521.

7. *Yalta Papers*, p. 677.

8. Ibid., p. 870.

9. Ibid., pp. 776-78.

10. Ibid., p. 804.

11. Ibid.

12. Ibid., pp. 842-43.

13. Ibid., p. 846.

14. Ibid., pp. 852-53.

15. Churchill (Matthews minutes): "In Parliament I must be able to say that the elections will be held in a fair way. I do not care much about Poles myself." (Ibid., p. 853.) Roosevelt: "I don't want the Poles to be able to question the Polish elections. The matter is not only one of principle but of practical politics." (Ibid., p. 854.)

16. Ibid., p. 872.

17. Churchill, *Triumph and Tragedy* (see chap. 3, note 5), p. 385.

18. The original American proposal (*Yalta Papers*, p. 863) included the phrasing "When, in the opinion of the three governments, conditions in any European liberated state or any former Axis satellite state in Europe make such action necessary, they will immediately *establish appropriate machinery for the carrying out* of the joint responsibilities set forth in this declaration." Molotov objected to this in the Foreign Ministers' meeting of February 10 and proposed that the paragraph, instead of speaking of establishing appropriate machinery, should end "will immediately *take measures for the carrying out of mutual consultation.*" (*Yalta Papers*, p. 873.) This is approximately the language reflected in the final document. In any case, the

words "when, in the opinion of *the three governments*" made it clear that unanimity would be required for this clause to become operative.

Herbert Feis (p. 550) comments on the Declaration for Liberated Europe: "It is hard to judge whether either Soviet or British governments shared the sense of the American formulators that its principles might govern events. Its loose net of phrases allowed easy passage to any determined purpose. The struggle within these countries was not just another chapter in Anglo-Soviet rivalry for influence in Europe. It was part of a world contest between those who looked to Moscow for leadership and those attached to other social ideas and systems. As long as that contest went on, coalition arrangements composed of such mutually hostile elements could be only temporary; and unless it was suspended, the resort to free elections, as the solvent of internal political differences, was certain to be impeded. What would happen if the people of one of the countries on the Soviet frontiers elected a government actively opposed to the Soviet Union? What if one of the countries in the West elected a Communist government? Looked at another way, the question was whether the Anglo-Soviet attempt to limit the struggle by a division of spheres of influence should be discarded for excellent political principles which might, however, in the circumstances, have wayward results."

McNeill comments: "The Americans conceived this Declaration as a sort of antidote to the 'spheres of influence' deal which Churchill and Stalin had concluded in October 1944. Tripartite responsibility and action in all areas of Europe was to be the pattern for the difficult period after the end of hostilities, and special spheres in which one or another of the Allies would have preeminent influence were to be abandoned. Stalin clearly had no such thought in mind when he accepted the Declaration. Perhaps he felt it a harmless piece of rhetoric, soothing to the Americans. After all, three-power action, by the terms of the Declaration, would occur only when all three of the Allies judged it necessary, and any one Power could always find any proposed action unnecessary if its own policies seemed to be called in question. . . ." Royal Institute of International Affairs, *America, Britain, and Russia—Their Cooperation and Conflict, 1941-1946,* by William Hardy McNeill (London: Oxford University Press, 1953), p. 559.

19. Cf. Captain Thorneycroft's speech in the House of Commons

on February 28, 1945, quoted in Norman A. Graebner, *Cold War Diplomacy: American Foreign Policy, 1945-1960* (Princeton, N.J.: Van Nostrand, 1962), Document No. 2, pp. 141-42, from which the following passages: "I concede at once—and this may be embarrassing for the Government—that I do not regard the Polish settlement as an act of justice. It may be right or wrong, it may be wise or foolish, but at any rate it is not justice as I understand the term. It is not the sort of situation in which you get two parties to a dispute putting their case forward in front of a disinterested body and in which the strength and power of one of the parties is never allowed to weigh in the balance. The sooner we recognize that we are a long way from that sort of thing happening the better.

"The Government had two choices only. They could have postponed the issue. . . . They could have said, 'No, we want this submitted to arbitration. We cannot do anything without the consent of the London Polish Government'. No one knows what would happen in those circumstances, but one can safely say that it is unlikely that there would in any circumstance be a free, independent and democratic Poland. The Red Army is in occupation of that country and the Lublin Committee is in control. . . . The second course that they could adopt was to make the best settlement they could and impose it deliberately on the Poles. . . .

"We have encouraged the London Polish Government to negotiate, and have criticized them because they did not negotiate very well. We have told them they must make concessions, and then we have blamed them because they did not make concessions. I do not regard that as a sensible or an honourable course. I do not believe you can ask a Pole to decide to hand over a half of his country. I do not think it is a fair thing to ask any Pole to do. If they agreed to do that, they would divide Poland for a generation, perhaps for all time, into those who thought they were patriots and those who thought they were traitors. This is to perpetuate civil war. Nor could you ask the Poles as an act of policy to take a large slice of their powerful neighboring State. . . . That is a decision which must be taken by more powerful States. I do not believe that you save your honour in this matter by imposing on others the obligation of making a decision which you ought to make yourself."

20. Göbbels in *Das Reich* of February 24, 1945: "Should the German people lay down their arms, the agreement between Roosevelt, Churchill and Stalin would allow the Soviets to occupy all East and Southeast Europe, together with the major part of the Reich. An iron curtain would at once descend on this territory which, including the Soviet Union, would be of enormous dimensions. Behind this curtain would begin a mass slaughter of the people, probably with the acclamation from the London and New York Jewish press. . . . The remainder of Europe would be engulfed in chaotic political and social confusion which would only represent a preparatory stage for the coming bolshevization."—Churchill's "iron curtain" speech at Fulton, Missouri, which popularized the term, was given on March 5, 1946. But Churchill had used the term "iron curtain" much earlier, in his message to President Truman of May 12, 1945. There is no evidence that the British leader was aware of Göbbels' earlier use of the term "iron curtain" to describe the division of Europe that was being created in early 1945 by Russian policy and military power.

21. Churchill, *Triumph and Tragedy*, p. 442.

22. *Stalin Correspondence* (see chap. 3, note 19), II, 200.

23. Ibid., II, 206.

24. Ibid., II, 209. The matter was somewhat awkward for the Western Allies because they had notified the Russians prior to sending officers to Berne to contact the German emissary. When the Russians demanded that three Soviet officers be also present at the interview, the Western Allies declined and went ahead with the preliminary contacts on their own, though promising to cut the Russians in as soon as actual negotiations would take place. Two other awkward features in subsequent developments of the affair, which might have come to the attention of Russian agents in Switzerland, were these: the German SS General Wolff, who said he could arrange for the surrender of General Kesselring's forces in Italy, continued to deal with Kesselring even after that general had been transferred from Italy to take command of the German forces on the Western Front. It was never satisfactorily explained why Wolff had to deal with the German commander of the Western Front if he was still trying to arrange only for the surrender of the German forces in Italy, which were now under General Vietinghoff. Furthermore, although

Wolff never returned to the subsequent place of contact in Switzerland where Allied officers had awaited him, his go-between (an Italian industrialist, Baron Parilli) made precisely the kind of proposal that Stalin suspected—that the Germans in Italy would not surrender themselves but would be granted the right to withdraw from Italy after the cessation of hostilities. But contrary to what Stalin suspected, that idea was not for a moment entertained by the Western Allies. Neither, however, was it explicitly rejected. Parilli was just told that if the Germans would send someone with full authority to Allied Force Headquarters, the draft copy of the capitulation would be handed to him there. (Cf. *The Italian Campaign, 12 December 1944 to 2nd May 1945: A Report to the Combined Chiefs of Staff by the Supreme Allied Commander Mediterranean, Field Marshall the Viscount Alexander of Tunis,* London, H.M. Stationery Office, 1951.)

25. *Stalin Correspondence,* II, 204. The last sentence of Stalin's message to which Roosevelt referred had responded to Roosevelt's warning that Molotov's absence from San Francisco would be construed all over the world as a lack of comparable interest in the great objectives of that Conference on the part of the Soviet government. Stalin's reply to this had been: "As to the different interpretations, you will appreciate that they cannot determine the decisions to be taken." Ibid., II, 200.

26. Ibid., II, 202-203.

27. *Stalin Correspondence,* I, 309-10. Churchill interpreted the Yalta decision as calling for both a "new" and "reorganized" Polish government. Technically he could point to the fact that the Protocol used the word "new" twice in describing the government that was to be created. When it came to describing *how* it was to be created, however, the Protocol spoke of "reorganizing" the Provisional Government (i.e. the Lublin group) by the "inclusion" of other Poles. Cf. text, p. ix above.

28. Feis, p. 575. The complete text has not yet been published. Mr. Feis had access to official U. S. files in the preparation of his book.

29. *Stalin Correspondence,* II, 211-12. It is interesting to note that the Russian interpretation of this feature of the Yalta Agreement was shared by the bitterly anti-Soviet London Polish government, which considered that the Big Three had accepted domination of the new

Provisional Government by the Lublin group. Cf. Jan Ciechanowski, *Defeat in Victory* (Garden City, N.Y.: Doubleday, 1947), p. 363: "When I told him [Stettinius] that the wording of the Yalta Agreement did not clearly state that an entirely 'new government' was to be formed but implied that a compromise government, dominated by the Lublin communists, had been accepted, Stettinius kept on insisting that this was not the case and that it was clearly understood among the Big Three that there was to be 'an entirely new government and not a reconstructed Lublin government.' "

30. Harry S. Truman, *Memoirs* (Garden City, N.Y.: Doubleday, 1955), I, 15.

31. *Stalin Correspondence*, II, 215-17.

32. Truman *Memoirs*, I, 77-79. Secretary Stimson, Admiral Leahy, and General Marshall counseled against toughness. Secretary Forrestal, Ambassador Harriman and General Deane (who commanded the Military Mission to the Soviet Union) were in favor of laying it on the line. Some excerpts convey the flavor of their positions as recorded by President Truman:

"Mr. Stimson . . . said he would like to know how far the Russian reaction to a strong position on Poland would go. He said he thought that the Russians perhaps were being more realistic than we were in regard to their own security. . . . Admiral Leahy . . . observed that he had left Yalta with the impression that the Soviet government had no intention of permitting a free government to operate in Poland and that he would have been surprised had the Russians behaved differently. In his opinion, the Yalta agreement was susceptible to two interpretations. He added that he felt it was a serious matter to break with the Russians but that he believed we should tell them that we stood for a free and independent Poland. . . . General Marshall said from the military point of view the situation in Europe was secure but that we hoped for Soviet participation in the war against Japan at a time when it would be useful to us. . . . He was inclined to agree with Mr. Stimson that the possibility of a break with Russia was very serious.

"Secretary Forrestal expressed the view that this difficulty over Poland could not be treated as an isolated incident—that there had been many evidences of the Soviet desire to dominate adjacent countries and to disregard the wishes of her allies. It was his belief that for some time the Russians had been under the impression that we would not object if they took over all of Eastern Europe, and he said it was his profound conviction that if the Russians were to be rigid in their attitude we had better have a showdown with them now rather than later. . . . Ambassador Harriman . . . said he felt that when Stalin and Molotov had returned from Moscow after Yalta they had learned more of the situation in Poland and had realized how shaky the provisional government was. On that account they had come to realize that the introduction of any genuine Polish leader such as Mikolajczyk would probably mean the elimination of the Soviet hand-picked crop of leaders. It was his belief, therefore, that the real issue was whether we were to be a party to a program of Soviet domination of Poland. He said obviously we were faced with the possibility of a break with the Russians, but he felt that, properly handled, it might still be avoided. . . . General Deane . . . said he was convinced after his experience in Moscow that if we were afraid of the Russians we would get nowhere, and he felt that we should be firm when we were right."

33. *Stalin Correspondence*, II, 218-19.

34. Truman *Memoirs*, I, 82.

35. *Stalin Correspondence*, II, 219-20.

36. Russell, (see note 5, above), pp. 636-37. The text of the Stettinius statement had been drafted by Senator Arthur H. Vandenberg.

37. Cf. note 5 to this chapter.

38. Churchill, *Triumph and Tragedy,* pp. 494-97.

39. The issue relating to discussion of a dispute in the absence of unanimity among the great powers was subsequently settled during Harry Hopkins' visit to Stalin. During that conversation, on June 6, it appeared that Molotov might not have adequately informed Stalin of the interpretation of the Yalta Agreement on voting procedure which he had defended in San Francisco. Cf. Robert E. Sherwood, *Roosevelt and Hopkins* (New York: Harper, 1948), p. 911.

40. *Stalin Correspondence*, II, 226-27.

41. The record of the fifth conversation between Stalin and Hopkins, in which these arrangements were made, has not yet been

published. Although Mikolajczyk referred to "three or four" of the five Poles from Poland as having been required by Stalin to be "sympathetic to the old Lublin Committee" (Stanislaw Mikolajczyk, *The Rape of Poland—Pattern of Soviet Aggression* [New York: McGraw-Hill, 1948], p. 114), actually only two of them were labeled by him as pro-Communist. However, this was sufficient to give the pro-Communists and their allies a clear majority. Mikolajczyk himself was among the Poles invited from London, as he had meanwhile made a public statement accepting the Yalta decisions on Poland, and he even became a member of the new Polish government; but he was effectively prevented from rallying the forces opposed to the Communists.

42. "These results," wrote McNeill (p. 588), "flowed centrally from the settlement of the Polish issue, and, though Stalin had yielded to the extent of admitting Mikolajczyk and some other non-Communist Poles within the pale, the Western Powers yielded far more. It was perhaps not perfectly clear at the time, but it was proved by subsequent events that Communist domination of the Polish Provisional Government survived the 'reorganization' for which Hopkins' mission had prepared the way; yet it was to prevent such domination that Britain and America had argued so long. Having won a clear path to his appointed goal—a 'friendly' government in Poland—Stalin was willing and anxious to conciliate the West on other issues, and it was doubtless this desire which accounted for the casualness with which he settled the dispute over the veto power on the Security Council. If the West would allow him to dominate Eastern Europe and Manchuria Stalin was willing to cooperate; but he clearly put Soviet interests in these border regions ahead of all other considerations."

43. *Potsdam Papers*, (see chap. 2, note 1), II, 206.

44. Ibid., II, 1123.

45. *Yalta Papers*, p. 781.

46. Cf. Arthur Bliss Lane, *I Saw Poland Betrayed* (New York: Bobbs-Merrill, 1948), Chapter 19.

5

Spheres of Influence

Less than two weeks after the Yalta Conference, the Russians flagrantly violated the spirit of the Declaration on Liberated Europe by forcing a Communist-dominated government upon Rumania. Andrei Vyshinsky, the Soviet deputy commissar for foreign affairs, flew to Bucharest and declared that the Soviet government had to see that order was maintained behind the front; that the government of General Radescu was incapable of maintaining order; and that a new government must be based on "the truly democratic forces of the country."[1] He gave King Michael two hours to inform the public that General Radescu had been dismissed. In leaving the King, Vyshinsky, according to official American reports, "slammed the door so hard that the plaster around the door frame was badly cracked." Vyshinsky next day informed King Michael that the Communist leader, Petru Groza, was the choice of the Soviet government, and he was quoted as saying that unless the King accepted Groza and his team "he would not be responsible for the continuance of Rumania as an independent state."[2]

In order to place this event in perspective, it is necessary to review the background of enemy countries that came under Allied occupation and the arrangements concerning them that had grown up during the war; for the situation in Rumania was totally different, for instance, from the situation in Poland. Poland was a country allied with Great Britain that had been first invaded by Russia and later "liberated" by Russia from the Germans. Rumania, on the other hand, was an ally of Germany, a Fascist-run country whose troops had participated in the invasion of Russia and had, as a matter of fact, shared in the occupation of Yalta and the Crimea until driven out by the Red Army. As we shall see, the situations in Yugoslavia and Hungary were different again. But we must go back quite a bit if we are to see the picture as a whole.

It will be recalled, first of all, that as early as 1942 Russia pressed for Western recognition of the principle that it should regain the boundaries of 1941 after the war; that the British had been inclined to concede this; but that the United States successfully interposed objections (cf. Chapter 3 and its note 10). Stalin's idea, already at that time, had been that Russia should be granted a special sphere of influence in eastern Europe, in return for which he was prepared to recognize British preeminence in the countries to be liberated in the West (cf. Chapter 3). This idea ran completely counter to American policy, which was to agree first on principles of general validity and to apply them to particular cases only when an orderly framework for international collaboration had been established. Spheres of influence, in particular, were abhorrent to Cordell Hull. He recalled in his memoirs: "I could sympathize fully with Stalin's desire to protect his western borders from future attack. But I felt that this security could best be obtained through a strong postwar peace organization."[3]

The first European country to be occupied by the advancing Allied armies was Italy, which capitulated to General Eisenhower's forces on September 3, 1943 under terms that acknowledged the authority of the Allied commander-in-chief to establish military government in Italy. General Smith signed the document, whose terms had been approved by the Russians, "by authority of the Governments of the United States and Great Britain and in the interest of the United Nations." The armistice agreement did not indicate which of the United Nations should take part in the work of supervising and controlling Italian affairs. But the Russian position on this point was indicated even before the armistice was signed. Stalin, on August 22, suggested activation of a "military-political commission" to deal jointly with problems of "various countries falling away from Germany," and he proposed that the commission be located in Sicily.[4] This suggestion was very poorly received by Roosevelt and Churchill, who learned of it while they were consulting in Quebec.[5]

Roosevelt tried to brush off Stalin's suggestion by pretending to misunderstand. He wrote the Soviet dictator: "Why not send an officer to General Eisenhower's headquarters in connection with the commission to sit in Sicily on further settlements with the Italians? He would join the British and Americans who are now working on this very subject."[6] But Stalin was not to be put off: "The despatch of a Soviet officer to General Eisenhower's headquarters," he replied immediately, "can in no way replace the military-political commission, which is required to direct on the spot negotiations with Italy and with the Governments of other countries falling away from Germany."[7] As it was impossible to deny the Russians any role at all, Roosevelt and Churchill agreed to the establishment of the Military-Political Commission—but in Algiers instead of Sicily, and with strictly circumscribed functions which would essentially confine the Russian representative to giving and receiving information.[8] The divergence became obvious when the Russians appointed Vyshinsky himself as their representative, while Roosevelt issued instructions to Eisenhower to set up a separate Control Commission for Italy under his direct command.[9]

The Russians immediately protested the establishment of the (U. S.–British) Control Commission, pointing to the existence of the (tripartite) Military-Political Commission to which they had just appointed a high-ranking representative. In the Russian view, the Commission in Algiers was to have a role in shaping political events in Italy and in guiding the military occupation. In the Western view, its function was purely advisory. In the end it was decided that an "Inter-Allied Advisory Council" should be established for Italy, but the Western Allies successfully insisted that their commander-in-chief must retain full and unrestricted authority. The Russians thus lost in their attempt to obtain an important role in influencing political events in Italy under Allied occupation. Vyshinsky, whose rank was now clearly excessive for an essentially advisory position, soon returned to Russia. Later, when an Allied Control Commission was set up in Rumania, and when the American and British governments asked for a share in determining occupation policies, Vyshinsky denied that request and referred to Italy as a precedent;[10] and the Russian chairman of the commission in Rumania pointed out that since the United States and Britain had made the executive decisions in Italy in the name of all the

United Nations, he felt entitled to do the same in Rumania.[11]

The capitulation of Italy had immediate repercussions in Greece, which had been largely garrisoned by Italian troops. As these troops were withdrawn, their arms found their way into the hands of Greek guerrilla fighters. While the Germans were able to recover control of the main cities and lines of communications in Greece, the war there from the fall of 1943 onward became a triangular affair: the Germans on the one hand, and on the other two Greek guerrilla organizations, ELAS and EDES, which at the same time fought each other. ELAS, the bigger organization, was republican and under strong Communist influence. EDES, although originally also republican, was opposed to the Communists and gradually attracted also conservative and royalist elements. The British in early 1944 tried to promote a truce among the Greek guerrillas. However, in March ELAS and its supporting political organizations, EAM (Greek initials for National Liberation Front), set up a provisional government which implicitly challenged the legitimacy of the Greek government-in-exile in Cairo. This situation had overtones reminiscent of the Polish issue, and it caused special concern to Churchill.

Meanwhile, in March 1944 the Red Army had entered Bessarabia, a province of Rumania which had been Russian territory from 1812 to 1917, which Russia had taken back in 1941, and which it now claimed as Russian territory—much in the manner in which it claimed Poland east of the Curzon Line. The Russians also claimed northern Bukovina, an area inhabited by Ukrainians which they had also taken over in 1941. (Perhaps because Rumania was an enemy whose consent was not required, disposition of these territories had not become an important issue in Russia's relations with its Western allies.) As the Russians were now poised on what they considered the true border of Rumania, they issued a public statement on April 2, 1944, disclaiming any intention of annexing Rumanian territory or of "changing the existing social order in Rumania." This statement was apparently designed to influence the Rumanian government to forsake its alliance with Hitler, and to reassure the Western powers about Russia's intentions in eastern Europe.[12] Both the American and British governments praised the Russian avowals.

But Churchill was far from reassured. With great difficulty he had just managed to remodel the Greek and Yugoslav governments-in-exile in such a manner that they seemed to have a chance of coming to acceptable terms with the resistance elements fighting in their countries; and he looked with concern at the prospect of Russian power and influence spreading into the Balkans. He was disquieted, furthermore, by the fact that the Russians in early May had declined to cooperate with him with regard to Greece.[13] He did not feel confident that the United States would support a strong stand in the Balkans, especially in view of President Roosevelt's often expressed distaste at the idea of American involvement in that part of Europe.[14] Although Churchill knew that the idea of spheres of influence was anathema to the American government, which equated it with the kind of power politics that had discredited the peace settlements after World War I, Churchill decided to take an initiative. On May 5 the British government suggested to the Russian ambassador in London an arrangement whereby Rumania would be considered to be in Russia's, and Greece in Britain's sphere of responsibility.

The Russians were willing to accept such a deal, but only if it had the blessing of the United States. This Churchill now tried to obtain.

Such an arrangement [he telegraphed Roosevelt] would be a natural development of the existing military situation, since Rumania falls within the sphere of the Russian armies and Greece within the Allied command under General Wilson in the Mediterranean. . . . I hope you may feel able to give this proposal your blessing. We do not of course wish to carve up the Balkans into spheres of influence, and in agreeing to the arrangement we should make it clear that it applied only to war conditions and did not affect the rights and responsibilities which each of the Great Powers will have to exercise at the peace settlement and afterwards in regard to the whole of Europe.[15]

When these views were presented to him by the British ambassador, Hull was flatly opposed. "It seemed to me," he later wrote, "that any creation of zones of influence would inevitably sow the seeds of future conflict. I felt that zones of influence could not but derogate from the over-all authority of the international security organizations which I expected would come into being."[16]

At first blush [Hull told Halifax] in view of the many charges and counter-charges now rising—and which will certainly rise in the future—about encroachments first by one Government and then by another on the economic, political, military, or other internal affairs of the Balkans and other European countries, it would be a doubtful course to abandon our broad basic declarations of policy, principles, and practice. If these are departed from in one or two important instances, such as you propose, then neither of the two countries parties to such an act will have any precedent to stand on, or any stable rules by which to be governed and to insist that other Governments be governed.[17]

Hull persuaded Roosevelt to reply to Churchill also in this sense.

118

Churchill was convinced that the American position was unrealistic, and he came back with another message to Roosevelt. "Action is paralysed," he wrote, "if everybody is to consult everybody else about everything before it is taken. Events will always outstrip the changing situations in these Balkan regions. Somebody must have the power to plan and act." He referred to a recent mutiny of the Greek forces of the government-in-exile which had been squelched by the British. "If in these difficulties we had had to consult other Powers and a set of triangular or quadrangular telegrams got started the only result would have been chaos or impotence. . . . The Russians are ready to let us take the lead in the Greek business, which means that EAM and all its malice can be controlled by the national forces of Greece. Otherwise civil war and ruin to the land you care about so much. . . ." He pointed out that the Russians were about to invade Rumania and that, "considering that neither you nor we have any troops there at all . . . they will probably do what they like anyhow." He pleaded that the arrangement with Russia be given a trial for three months.[18]

In a separate message to Lord Halifax, which the British ambassador conveyed to Hull, Churchill made some important additional points. First, he said, "it seems reasonable that the Russians should deal with the Rumanians and Bulgarians, upon whom their armies are impinging"—thus indicating that in his view the arrangement should also extend to Bulgaria. He felt, on the other hand, that British primacy with respect to Greece should also extend to Yugoslavia. And he added, archly: "On the other hand, we follow the lead of the United States in South America as far as possible, as long as it is not a question of our beef and mutton. On this we naturally develop strong views on account of the little we get."[19] In other words, Churchill was pointing out that the United States, in effect, had its own sphere of influence in Latin America. In the end, Roosevelt profited from the temporary absence of Hull from Washington to risk the wrath of his secretary of state by approving the deal on a three-month try-out basis and with the admonition that "we must be careful to make it clear that we are not establishing any post-war spheres of influence."[20]

Although the British told the Russians that they had received a green light from Washington, the Russians decided that they should check directly with the American government to make sure that there was no misunderstanding. By this time, however, Hull was back on the job. With the President's approval he replied confirming that the United States had agreed to the arrangement on a three-month trial basis, but he took the occasion to express the American misgivings about the project at such length and so insistently that Stalin seems to have lost interest in it.[21] In any event, Churchill pleaded in vain with Stalin to give the arrangement a try.[22] But the American note, which had indicated that any British-Russian arrangements "would have neither direct nor indirect validity as affecting the interests of this Government," clearly deprived it of most of its value to the Russians.[23]

The question of spheres thus remained in suspense during the summer of 1944. We have seen that the Russians were poised on the borders of prewar Rumania in April 1944 and that Churchill had managed in May to reorganize the Greek government-in-exile in a manner that seemed to promise the establishment of a truly representative coalition government when Greece would be liberated. In June 1944 the British pressed King Peter of Yugoslavia to appoint a prime minister (Ivan Subasic) who on his part might be able to work with the partisan leader, Tito. The British government clearly was looking for political leaders from eastern and southeastern Europe who would be non-Communist and yet able to work with the Communists on a basis that would make those countries not basically anti-Russian, as they had been before the war. In Greece and Yugoslavia Churchill thought that he had found such a solution. In Czechoslovakia, Beneš seemed to symbolize the same pattern. But in Poland and Rumania it was impossible to work out a compromise.

During the summer months, as the Western Allies broke out of their beachhead in Normandy and the Russian armies mounted their massive offensives in Poland, the Germans moved some of their best divisions out of Rumania. Thereupon, in August, the Red Army finally launched an offensive on that front. The King of Rumania now ousted the Fascist government of the pro-German dictator, Antonescu, and installed a coalition regime of representatives of four parties: the National Peasants, led by the popular conservative, Iuliu Maniu; the Liberals, under Dinu Bratianu; the small Socialist Party; and the even smaller Communist Party. This new government, headed by General Sanatescu, signed an armistice with Russia on September 12 under which it joined the fight against Germany. Contrary to the pattern in Poland, the Russians did not arrive in Rumania with a preformed government of their own but seemed content, at least for the time being, to work with the new coalition government, in which the Communists were clearly in a minority.

The Rumanian armistice also provided that "an Allied Control Commission will be established which will undertake until the conclusion of peace the regulation of and control over the execution of the present terms under the general direction and orders of the Allied (Soviet) High Command acting on behalf of the Allied powers." Molotov made it plain to the United

States and Britain that the Soviet High Command alone would have authority to issue orders to the Rumanian government; that the Soviet member on the Control Commission would exercise executive power for the Commission; and that the functions of the British and American members would be what the Soviet government regarded as analogous to those of the Soviet representatives attached to the Control Commission in Italy. The United States remonstrated for a while, but in the end had to go along with these provisions.[24]

The next country to fall to the Russians was Bulgaria. When Rumania capitulated, the pro-German government in Bulgaria resigned, and its successor at first attempted to follow a policy of neutrality while announcing that it would carry on negotiations with the United States and Great Britain for an armistice and that it would seek "the most sincere relations founded on trust with fraternal Russia." But Russia insisted on more. On September 5 Russia declared war against Bulgaria, and on September 9, after a new government had come into office in Sofia and had declared war against Germany, hostilities by Russia were suspended. The new Bulgarian government was much more heavily weighted in favor of the Communists than the government in Rumania, largely because the Communists had been active as partisans and the Bulgarians in general did not harbor the traditional fears of Russia that existed in Rumania. The preliminary armistice agreement with Bulgaria provided for an Allied Control Commission which clearly lodged action responsibility in the "Allied (Soviet) High Command."[25]

Meanwhile, the British efforts to produce moderate coalition regimes in Greece and Yugoslavia were affected by the Russian advance into the Balkans. In Greece, a Russian military mission to ELAS made its appearance in July 1944.[26] For some reason, however, the Russians seemed to keep to the spirit of the abortive agreement with Great Britain and refrained from lending active support to ELAS. In August Churchill had an interview with the premier of the Greek government-in-exile, Georgios Papandreou, and apparently concluded that he was suited to conciliate the Communist-led resistance movement in Greece without letting it take power in the country. The EAM now decided to join the Papandreou government, and in September an agreement was concluded whereby both the Greek government-in-exile and the two rival undergrounds, EDES and ELAS, recognized the military authority of the Supreme Allied Commander in the Mediterranean, General Wilson, and accepted his appointment of a British general to exercise command in Greece.[27] The stage was set for a British landing in Greece. Would the Communist-led ELAS live up to the agreement and submit to British control? Or would the British have to intervene in a civil war? It seemed to depend, in no small measure, on the position of the Soviet Union.

If Greece was an enemy-occupied country waiting to be liberated, Yugoslavia was a country that in 1944 had very large indigenous forces in the field against the Germans. Marshal Tito, who enjoyed both Russian and British support, was in control of a major part of his country. As in Greece, the future status of the monarchy was a burning political issue. In August Churchill met with Tito in Italy and attempted to effect a reconciliation between him and King Peter. During this period, the Yugoslav partisans were still dependent on the British in Italy for some logistical support, but on September 6 Tito's forces established contact with the advancing Red Army and Britain's bargaining position with Tito correspondingly declined. Later in September Tito flew to Moscow, where, as was much later revealed, Stalin urged him to let King Peter return to Yugoslavia.[28] An agreement was also concluded whereby Tito's National Committee of Liberation would conduct the civil administration of any Yugoslav territory occupied by the Red Army. To Churchill all this again looked most ominous, involving the projection of Russian power into the Mediterranean. The United States was of little help to him because, while it insisted on a policy based on high principles, it refused to get itself involved in eastern European affairs, especially prior to the 1944 elections.[29]

Churchill now decided to go to Moscow and discuss the whole range of problems of east and southeast Europe with Stalin even though Roosevelt, preoccupied with domestic politics, was unable to participate. Churchill arrived in Moscow on October 9 and during his first private meeting with Stalin immediately drove to the heart of the matter. As he recalls: "The moment was apt for business, so I said, 'Let us settle about our affairs in the Balkans. Your armies are in Rumania and Bulgaria. We have interests, missions, and agents there. Don't let us get at cross-purposes in small ways. So far as Britain and Russia are concerned, how would it do for you to have ninety per cent predominance in Rumania, for us to have ninety per cent of the say in Greece, and go fifty-fifty about Yugoslavia?' "[30] While this was being translated, Churchill wrote out on a sheet of paper the proportions he envisaged for Russia and "the others": Rumania 90:10, Greece 10:90, Yugoslavia and Hungary 50:50, Bulgaria 75:25.[31]

"I pushed this across to Stalin, who had by then heard the translation," Churchill recalls. "There was a slight pause. Then he took his blue pencil and made a large tick upon it, and passed it back to us. It was all settled in no more time than it takes to set down. . . . After this there was a long silence. The pencilled paper lay in the centre of the table. At length I said, 'Might it not be thought rather cynical if it seemed we had disposed of these issues, so fateful to millions of people, in such an offhand manner? Let us burn the paper.' 'No, you keep it,' said Stalin."[32]

The deal was made. What was the attitude of the United States toward it? Here, once more, a distinction must be made between the position of President Roosevelt and that of his most important subordinates. Before Churchill went to Moscow, he informed the President in general terms of what he intended to discuss. The President dispatched—or thought he dispatched— a message to Churchill giving his general blessing to the forthcoming talks and suggesting only that Ambassador Harriman be also present. However, when Hopkins learned of that message he feared that it would give the impression that the United States was washing its hands of the Balkans and letting Churchill make commitments also in its name. As reported by Sherwood, "Hopkins immediately investigated and learned that this cable was already going out over the wires of the Map Room. He thereupon took one of the quick and arbitrary actions, far beyond the scope of his own authority, which had gained for him the admiration and affection of Roosevelt ever since the beginnings of the New Deal: he gave orders to the officers on duty in the Map Room that transmission of the President's message to Stalin was to be stopped. . . . Hopkins then went straight to Roosevelt's bed room—the President was shaving at the time —and told what he had done and the reasons why he had done it."[33] He persuaded Roosevelt to send a message to Stalin instead, of a totally different tenor:

"There is in this global war literally no question, either military or political," the message drafted by Hopkins and Bohlen read, "in which the United States is not interested. You will naturally understand this. It is my firm conviction that the solution to still unsolved questions can be found only by the three of us together. Therefore, while I appreciate the necessity for the present meeting, I choose to consider your forthcoming talks with Mr. Churchill merely as preliminary to a conference of the three of us which can take place, so far as I am concerned, any time after our national election." In a separate message to Ambassador Harriman, Roosevelt asked him to bear in mind that there could be "no subjects that I can anticipate that might be discussed between Stalin and the Prime Minister in which I will not be greatly concerned. It is important that I retain complete freedom of action after this conference is over."[34] Still, when the British-Russian deal was made the United States this time did not remonstrate, and Roosevelt even sent a vague greeting to Churchill and Stalin that might have been interpreted as a blessing.[35]

In any event, the deal went into effect and it had immediate favorable consequences for the British position in the Balkans. They were given a free hand in Greece and, as we shall see, used it with determination. With respect to Yugoslavia, Churchill and Stalin announced that they were going to try to bring about a union between the Yugoslav government-in-exile and Tito's National Liberation movement, and they sent a joint message to Tito and Subasic urging them to meet again and work out their problems together. For Bulgaria they completed armistice terms which involved some slight improvements as compared to the situation in Rumania.[36] Most remarkably, Stalin now encouraged Churchill to move British troops into northwestern Yugoslavia and thence in the direction of Vienna.[37] This was a strategy which Churchill had favored at the Tehran conference, where Stalin had discouraged it.[38] Stalin knew that Tito was opposed to such a British landing, and historians are still divided as to why he now approved the idea and even urged it on the British premier.[39] (As it turned out, Churchill was unable—once more—to persuade the American Chiefs of Staff to approve the operation.[40])

British troops arrived in Athens in October, bringing the Papandreou government with them. That government, it will be remembered, was a coalition including representatives of the leftist and republican EAM, the political organization of the increasingly Communist-dominated ELAS underground. But when the Papandreou government now demanded that the guerrilla forces be disbanded, the EAM members resigned, a general strike was called, there were street demonstrations on December 3, and shortly thereafter the ELAS troops began a general insurrection. Churchill immediately ordered the local British commander, General Scobie, to intervene. In a telegram to him, he wrote: "You are responsible for maintaining order in Athens and for neutralizing or destroying all EAM-ELAS bands approaching the city. You may make any regulations you like for the strict control of the streets or for the rounding up of any number of truculent persons. . . . Do not . . . hesitate to act as if you were in a conquered city where a local rebellion is in progress."[41] As Churchill later wrote of this message, he had to admit that it was somewhat strident in tone, but he felt it so necessary to give a strong lead to the military commander that he intentionally worded it in the sharpest terms.[42]

The fighting at first went very badly for the British. The ELAS troops overran most of Athens and in fact overwhelmed their Greek opponents everywhere in the country with the exception of a few square miles in the capital and part of Salonika. There was bitter house-to-house fighting in Athens, and by December 11 Field Marshal Alexander telegraphed, "The British forces are in fact beleaguered in the heart of the city."[43] Massive British reinforcements were brought in from Italy and the Middle East, but Alexander warned that even with those added troops the British would be unable to control all of Greece. To make matters worse, the British action seemed to many in the West as an oppressive and reactionary move against men who had fought bravely against the Germans, and as a stifling of the people's will. Both in Britain and in the United States most of the press condemned the intervention in scathing terms.

Simultaneously, political crises blew up in Italy and Belgium. In Italy the government had fallen and it was proposed to reorganize it with Count Carlo Sforza as foreign minister. Sforza, however, was *persona non grata* with Churchill because of his failure to support the King of Italy at a time (in 1943) when he had promised the British premier to do so. Britain thus vetoed his inclusion in the new government. In Belgium, British troops were called out to prevent a Communist-led demonstration. As in Greece, the question of the future of the monarchy was there mingled with the question of disarming ex-resistance organizations. Thus in three European countries—Greece, Italy, and Belgium—where the British exercised primacy serious political crises broke out, and in each country the British position seemed to be in support of the monarchy and the more conservative elements against republicans and radicals. Churchill's position was made particularly difficult because the American government, in a formal statement by Stettinius, dissociated itself from the British actions in Italy and Greece.[44] Still worse, the prime minister's message to General Scobie leaked out to an American newspaper columnist and seemed to confirm the British action in Greece as high-handed and oppressive.[45]

But Churchill stood his ground. He could afford to conduct a farsighted, though momentarily unpopular, policy because he had charge not only of his party but of a coalition government and needed to fear no elections until after victory had been achieved.[46] Before his Parliament he insisted that Britain was defending not a particular regime but the right of the Greek people to decide freely, under conditions of normal tranquillity, whether their government was to be of the Left or of the Right. He put the question of confidence and was sustained, but by a discouraging margin. On Christmas Day 1944 he flew to Athens and, while he' was unable to bring the warring Greek factions together, he obtained their agreement to the installation of a Regent pending settlement of the constitutional question. (Roosevelt helped by pushing the King to accept this arrangement.) Meanwhile, British troops in Greece were increased to 60,000 and they finally went on the offensive. When Papandreou resigned and General Plastiras, a republican, succeeded him, the British position was also considerably improved. At the same time, a widespread reaction against the terrorism of ELAS in Athens also undermined the power of the insurgents. Finally, on January 14, 1945, a cease-fire was negotiated; and on February 12 a definite peace was arranged whereby ELAS agreed to disband and surrender its arms in return for a guarantee of amnesty.

Throughout this episode, the Russians remained completely quiet. Stalin, as Churchill noted, "adhered strictly and faithfully to our agreement of October, and during all the long weeks of fighting the Communists in the streets of Athens not one word of reproach came from *Pravda* or *Isvestia*."[47] Later, at Yalta, Stalin went out of his way to tell Churchill that "he had no intention of criticizing British policy in Greece."[48] With mock solicitude, he even offered Churchill assurances that a suggested Russian amendment to the Declaration on Liberated Europe, whereby the signatories would have been obligated to "support . . . political leaders of those countries who have taken an active part in the struggle against the German invaders" was not designed to apply to Greece.[49] Churchill on his part said that there had been a rather rough time in Greece and "they were very much obliged to Marshal Stalin for not having taken too great an interest in Greek affairs."[50]

Our narrative has now carried us, though by a different route, again to the Yalta Conference in February 1945. We have already noted that Greece was not a matter of contention there. Neither was Rumania. The British tried to bring up the situation in Bulgaria and Hungary, to make clear that they considered that after the conclusion of hostilities the three Great Powers should have an equal say in the administration of those countries, but time prevented the matter from being discussed.[51] On the other hand, there was some discussion of Yugoslavia, where Britain strove to maintain its 50:50 position of influence. In November 1944 Tito and Subasic had agreed to set up a three-man regency, pending a plebiscite to decide whether King Peter was to come back. However, the two Yugoslav leaders were unable to agree on the composition of that regency council. Moreover, the Yugoslav Communist leader was proclaiming his intention of annexing Trieste and a part of Austria, and Churchill was fearful that this might involve a head-on collision with the British, who were to occupy the disputed areas.

At Yalta Stalin repeated the suggestion which he had made to Churchill in October, that some British troops be transferred from the Italian front to Yugoslavia, whence they should be directed toward Vienna.[52] (Again, the American military leaders refused to entertain the idea.) Churchill proposed some amendments to the Tito-Subasic agreement, and Stalin agreed that those amendments—designed to improve the democratic base of the prospective coalition government—should be jointly urged upon the two Yugoslav leaders by the Big Three. After some hesitation, Roosevelt agreed to go along. The three also agreed to urge Tito and Subasic to get on with implementation of their agreement to form a coalition government. Thus at Yalta there was also no disagreement on Yugoslavia. It is perhaps significant, however, that Stalin claimed he had little influence upon Tito.[53] Churchill questioned this, but subsequent events seem to have shown that Stalin may have been telling the truth.

At the second plenary meeting in Yalta, President Roosevelt also made a remark which Churchill was to label a "momentous statement."[54] He said that he did not believe that American troops would stay in Europe much more than two years after the war. He felt that he could obtain support in Congress and throughout the country for any reasonable measures designed to safeguard the future peace, the President said, but he did not believe that this would extend to the maintenance of an appreciable American force in Europe.[55] It is not recorded what Stalin's reaction to this statement may have been. In any case, it is in this setting and against the background of the Polish issue detailed in Chapters 3 and 4, that the Declaration on Liberated Europe was agreed; and it is against the background of the agreements and disagreements on Rumania, Greece, Bulgaria, Hungary, and Yugoslavia set forth in the present chapter that one must view the violations of the Declaration by the Soviet Union which followed upon Yalta. We have already mentioned the unilateral forceful action taken by the Russians in Rumania. Many other Western grievances accumulated during the period between Yalta and Potsdam.

The Tito-Subasic agreement soon resulted not in a balancing of East and West but in a complete subjection of the Yugoslav conservatives by the Communists. The steps to enlarge the legislative body which had been urged by the Yalta Conference were never taken. "I must also say," wrote Churchill to Stalin on April 28, when he addressed the Russian dictator in the Polish matter,

> that the way things have worked out in Yugoslavia certainly does not give me the feeling of a fifty-fifty interest as between our countries. Marshal Tito has become a complete dictator. He has proclaimed that his prime loyalties are to the Soviet Union. Although he allowed members of the Royal Yugoslav Government to enter his government, they only number six as against twenty-five of his own nominees. We have the impression that they are not taken into consultation on matters of high policy and that it is becoming a one-party regime. However . . . I do not complain of any action you have taken there in spite of my misgivings and I hope it will all work out smoothly and make Yugoslavia into a prosperous and free people friendly to both Russia and ourselves.[56]

Territorial questions, which were supposed to await the peace settlements, began to bedevil the alliance. As a means of strengthening the Rumanian Communist Party, the Russians let it be known in January 1945 that they would return Transylvania to Rumania if the Communist-dominated "National Democratic Front" came to power; and on March 10, just four days after Groza took office, they extended Rumanian administration to that area which Hitler had awarded to Hungary. The unilateral extension of Polish administration to the Western Neisse has already been mentioned in Chapter 4. But the most vexing territorial issue concerned the Italian province of Venezia Giulia, where a substantial proportion of the population was ethnically Yugoslav (Croat and Slovene). Tito's forces swarmed into this area in April and were eventually confronted by British troops under General Alexander's command. Another Greece seemed in the making, and Churchill urged Truman to cooperate in forceful action to deny the strategic port of Trieste to the Yugoslavs.

"The great thing is to be there before Tito's guerrillas are in occupation," Churchill wrote the American President. "Therefore it does not seem to me there is a minute to wait. The actual status of Trieste can be determined at leisure. Possession is nine points of the law. I beg you for an early decision."[57] Truman hesitated to allow American troops to be committed, so Churchill authorized Alexander to go ahead using only British divisions. The dispute over Venezia Giulia was to last for many years, but by mid-1945 at least bloodshed between British and Yugoslav troops was avoided by an agreement on June 9. Stalin seemed to support the Yugoslav position, but the dispute between Yugoslavia and the Soviet Union three years later has brought out that Tito was in fact very much displeased by Stalin's failure to back him all the way in Trieste.[58] Churchill's disenchantment with the spheres-of-influence situation in Yugoslavia was recorded in his message to Stalin of June 23: "Our joint idea at the Kremlin in October was that the Yugoslav business should work out around 50-50 Russian and British influence. In fact it is at present more like 90-10, and even in that poor 10 we have been subjected to violent pressure by Marshal Tito."[59] From subsequent evidence, however, it appears that it was perhaps not Stalin who was pushing Tito but the reverse.

We have now accounted for the situation in Rumania, which —like Poland—was a country neighboring upon Russia, a country in which anti-Russian conservatives had predominated, from which Russia took back territory it had previously possessed, and in which Russia installed a completely Communist-dominated government;[60] Bulgaria, where the Communists were given a preponderant position which may initially have been

133

based, at least in part, on friendlier feelings toward Russia and on the anti-German record of Communist guerrillas—a position which the Communists gradually expanded by pressure and terror as 1945 wore on; Greece, where the Communists were beaten down by Britain with the acquiescence of Russia; and Yugoslavia, where British-Russian efforts to bring about a coalition between Communists and middle-class parties resulted only in a government clearly dominated by Tito's national Communist partisans, who had obtained control of their country largely by their own efforts. It remains to say a few words about Hungary and Czechoslovakia to explain why Communist domination there did not become an issue until long after 1945.

When Russian troops crossed into Hungary in October 1944, Admiral Horthy, the "regent" and strong man of Hungary, announced his intention of surrendering to the Red Army—but he was forestalled by a German coup and taken to a German concentration camp. However, a part of the Hungarian army under General Miklos surrendered to the Russians, and based on these elements the Russians installed a Provisional Hungarian Government at Debrecen, in eastern Hungary, in December 1944. The Allies negotiated an armistice with that government, with provisions along the lines of those for Bulgaria, giving the Soviet High Command the control power. The armistice also imposed very substantial reparations on Hungary, but at American insistence the Soviets agreed to scale these down by almost one-half.[61] By November the Red Army reached the outskirts of Budapest, but Hitler sent reinforcements to Hungary which halted the Russian offensive. It was not until April 1945, long after Yalta, that the German army was completely cleared out of the country.

The political organization in the Soviet-controlled part of Hungary, meanwhile, developed completely differently from what had occurred in Rumania, Bulgaria, and Yugoslavia. An underground "Hungarian Front" composed of Communists, Social Democrats, and the conservative Smallholders Party had agreed that those parties would establish a coalition after the war. The Debrecen government with Soviet permission allotted each of the three parties two cabinet posts, with others going to exponents of additional non-Communist groups. During the first months of the coalition the Communists cooperated genuinely with the other parties in preparing and carrying out certain fundamental economic and social changes which were agreed to be long overdue.[62] Most important among these was a land reform in March 1945 by which the huge feudal estates were broken up and over 600,000 peasants received land of their own.[63] The Communist minority position continued long after the Potsdam Conference. Although this takes us beyond the scope of this narrative, it may be noted that surprisingly free elections took place in Hungary under Soviet occupation in November 1945, in which the Smallholders obtained a smashing majority.[64] Nobody knows, of course, whether there was any connection between these free elections and the Churchill-Stalin agreement of 1944 which had assigned to Russia only a 50 per cent interest in Hungary. (The Soviet-engineered Communist take-over of Hungary took place only in 1947.)

If Hungary had been an enemy state, Czechoslovakia was an ally that had maintained a government-in-exile in London throughout the war but one which, in contrast to the Polish government-in-exile, had excellent relations with both Britain and Russia. President Edvard Beneš went to Moscow in December 1943 and there concluded a treaty of mutual assistance with the Soviet Union in which each pledged to act after the war "in accordance with the principles of mutual respect for the independence and sovereignty, as well as of non-interference in the internal affairs, of the other state."[65] It was also agreed that as Russian forces entered Czechoslovakia, they would be accompanied by Czech troops and the liberated areas would be progressively handed over to the Czechoslovak civil administration. When the Red Army entered Czechoslovakia in force, Benes arrived from London via Moscow to establish a provisional government in Slovakia in April 1945. In that government, which arrived in Prague in May, the Communists held seven out of twenty-five cabinet posts. This situation was analogous to that existing in most former German-occupied areas in western Europe[66] and did not give grounds for immediate concern in England and the United States.

Czechoslovakia had a tradition of friendliness and cultural affinity with Russia, which was of course totally absent in Poland and Rumania although it was paralleled to some extent in Bulgaria and Yugoslavia. Friendly feelings toward Russia had been heightened when Great Britain and France had sold out Czechoslovakia at Munich in 1938 over the protests of the Soviet Union. When Russia after the war asked Czechoslovakia to cede its easternmost tip, Ruthenia (also called Carpatho-Russia), which was largely inhabited by Ukrainians, this matter created no issue and the cession was amicably accomplished in June 1945, thereby completing the political unification of all Ukrainian lands within the frontiers of the Soviet Union[67] and giving Russia a common frontier with Hungary. Free elections were held in Czechoslovakia in 1946. (It was not until two years later that the Communists, by terror tactics and aided by Russian pressure, took over the country.)

This, then, completes our account of how the Russians came into eastern and southeastern Europe in the later stages of the war, and how British and Russian policies interacted in those areas. We have seen (Chapters 2 and 4) how the West opposed Russian predominance in Poland after Yalta on the basis of the ambiguous compromise that had been reached at that conference. It remains to review, again very briefly, the Western attitude toward Russian predominance in southeastern Europe. This attitude, too, was based on the Yalta agreements, in this case on the Declaration on Liberated Europe (page viii, Chapter 4). Any hope of reversing the process of increasing Russian influence and control depended in mid-1945 on the Western ability to make the Russians facilitate the holding of truly free elections. Any hope of the Soviet Union to maintain its control depended on the avoidance of such elections, especially in Rumania, where, as in Poland, the anti-Russian and anti-Communist sentiment was clearly overwhelming.

"Although I have in mind primarily the difficulties which the Polish negotiations have encountered," Roosevelt wrote Stalin on April 1, 1945, shortly before his death, "I must make a brief mention of our agreement embodied in the Declaration on Liberated Europe. I frankly cannot understand why the recent developments in Rumania should be regarded as not falling within the terms of that agreement. I hope you will find time personally to examine the correspondence between our Governments on this subject."[68] Stalin, on the other hand, pressed Churchill and Truman to extend diplomatic recognition to the Rumanian and Bulgarian governments on the ground that those countries had broken with the Axis and entered the war on the Allied side.[69] Truman's reply was crisp: he was disturbed, he said, to find governments in Rumania and Bulgaria "which do not accord to all democratic elements of the people the rights of free expression and which in their administration are, in my opinion, neither representative of nor responsive to the will of the people."[70] He asked that the U. S. S. R., Britain and the U. S.

concert their policies, i.e., bring about agreed changes in those countries. And there the matter rested until the Potsdam Conference in July 1945.

In President Truman's briefing book, which he studied on the way to Potsdam, was a document which succinctly summarized the situation in eastern Europe as it then existed. The relevant paragraph read:

> The Russians have taken steps to solidify their control over eastern Europe. They have concluded bilateral treaties of alliance with the Lublin Poles (in spite of our objections) and with the Governments of Yugoslavia and Czechoslovakia. They have taken unilateral action with respect to the formation of an Austrian Government, and have acted independently in Rumania, Bulgaria, and Hungary without consultation with the American and British representatives in those countries. An exclusive economic agreement has been concluded with Rumania which makes possible extensive Soviet control over Rumanian industry and which may virtually cut off Rumanian trade with the rest of the world. The Russians have rejected British and American proposals that discussions should take place regarding the political situation in Rumania and elections in Bulgaria. These actions are not in accordance with the Crimea Declaration on Liberated Europe whereby the Big Three were to concert their policies in assisting the liberated peoples to solve their pressing political and economic problems by democratic means. Eastern Europe is, in fact, a Soviet sphere of influence.[71]

At the Potsdam Conference, the United States introduced a document which called attention to the fact that the Yalta Declaration on Liberated Europe had not been carried out; called for reorganization of the Rumanian and Bulgarian governments; and proposed joint supervision ("assistance") of free elections in all the liberated territories.[72] The United States also proposed that the armistice for Italy be eased and that that nation be admitted to the United Nations. Churchill was unenthusiastic about this latter proposal. Stalin first tried to turn Churchill against the American position on Rumania and Bulgaria by privately pointing out to him that he was "not meddling in Greek affairs."[73] When this did not work, the Russians introduced a counter-document which defended the situation in Rumania and Bulgaria and blasted the situation in Greece "where law is not respected, where terrorism rages directed against democratic elements which have borne the principal burden of the fight against German invaders. . . ," etc.[74] This produced quite an uproar, in the course of which the Western representatives pointed out that the Greeks had welcomed supervision of their elections and that the international press was free to observe there, whereas Rumania and Bulgaria were cut off from the world.[75]

Secretary of State Byrnes records in his memoirs how he tried to make Molotov understand that Western insistence on free elections in eastern Europe was not intended to be an infringement of Russian interests: "The United States," he recalls saying to the Soviet commissar,

> sincerely desires Russia to have friendly countries on her borders, but we believe they should seek the friendship of the people rather than of any particular government. We, therefore, want the governments to be representative of the people. If elections are held while there are restrictions not only on newspaper and radio correspondents but upon our own governmental representatives as well, the American people will distrust any government established as a result of such an election. We do not wish to become involved in the elections of any country, but, because of the postwar situation, we would join with others in observing elections in Italy, Greece, Hungary, Rumania and Bulgaria.[76]

In the end, although the United States was prepared to substitute the word "observation" for "supervision," Stalin obdurately opposed any decision in the matter of free elections. In a moment of frankness he put the Soviet stand with unusual clarity as well as finality: "A freely elected government in any of these countries," he said, "would be anti-Soviet, and that we cannot allow."[77] When the British complained about the situation in Yugoslavia, the Russians again countered by introducing a paper lambasting Greece. Finally, Foreign Minister Bevin proposed that the papers on both Yugoslavia and Greece be withdrawn, and Stalin agreed with alacrity.[78] As a result, the Potsdam Conference brought no free elections in Rumania or Bulgaria and no change whatever in the division of eastern Europe as it had occurred at the end of the war on the basis of the power relationships as they existed at the time.

NOTES

1. James F. Byrnes, *Speaking Frankly* (New York: Harper, 1947), pp. 51-52.

2. Ibid.

3. *The Memoirs of Cordell Hull* (New York: Macmillan, 1948), II, 1170.

4. *Stalin Correspondence* (see chap. 3, note 19), I, 149.

5. Herbert Feis, *Churchill, Roosevelt, Stalin—The War They Waged and the Peace They Sought* (Princeton, N.J.: Princeton University Press, 1957), p. 172, reports that Roosevelt after receiving Stalin's message "came into the room before dinner saying, 'We are both mad'; and they were. . . . Though Eden and Ismay tried to get [Churchill] to take an easier view of the episode, he would not listen

to any excusing talk. After dinner, talking with Harriman, he remarked gloomily that he foresaw 'bloody consequences in the future' (using the word 'bloody' in its literal sense); and that he thought Stalin an unnatural man—with whom there would be grave trouble."

6. *Stalin Correspondence*, II, 89.

7. Ibid., II, 90.

8. Ibid., I, 154; II, 92. Churchill's description of the terms of reference was somewhat more restrictive than Roosevelt's.

9. "The pattern of Allied control over Italy which thus finally emerged lasted until the end of the war. It was of importance not only for Italy itself, but as a model for other armistice regimes in ex-enemy countries of Eastern Europe. Having excluded Russia from any but nominal participation in Italian affairs, the Western Powers prepared the way for their own exclusion from any but a marginal share in the affairs of Eastern Europe. No other arrangement, of course, conformed to the real distribution of military power and responsibility, or could have been compatible with the mutual distrust which lay close to the surface of Anglo-Russian and, less obviously, in the background of Russo-American relations." Royal Institute of International Affairs, *America, Britain and Russia—Their Cooperation and Conflict, 1941-1946,* by William Hardy McNeill (London: Oxford University Press, 1953), p. 310.

10. Feis, p. 416. Cf. also note 24 to this chapter.

11. Feis, pp. 546-47.

12. The Rumanian government had in fact shown signs of wishing to come to terms with the United Nations, but they were so afraid of the Russians that they insisted that British or American troops be sent into Rumania to counterbalance the Red Army; and this condition had not been accepted. Cf. William D. Leahy, *I Was There* (New York: Whittlesey House, 1950), p. 267.

13. Winston Churchill, *Closing the Ring* (see chap. 3, note 5), p. 551.

14. Hull *Memoirs,* II, 1612.

15. Churchill, *Triumph and Tragedy* (see chap. 3, note 5), pp. 73-74.

16. Hull *Memoirs,* II, 1452.

17. Ibid.

18. Churchill, *Triumph and Tragedy,* pp. 75-76.

19. Ibid., pp. 74-75.

20. Hull learned of the President's approval of the spheres-of-responsibility arrangements only through a telegram from the American ambassador to Greece, who was stationed in Cairo. He described his reaction: "I wrote the President a letter, enclosing a copy of Ambassador MacVeagh's telegram, and asking him whether any changes had been made in our position. The President replied on June 30, simply enclosing paraphrases or extracts of the messages which had been exchanged between himself and Mr. Churchill. These included his message of acceptance of June 12, to which Mr. Churchill had replied two days later expressing his deep gratitude and stating that he had asked Eden to convey the information to Molotov and make clear that the three months' limitation had been agreed to so that there would be no prejudgment of the question of establishing postwar spheres of influence." Hull *Memoirs,* II, 1456.

21. The Russian inquiry was dated July 1, 1944. The U. S. reply, dated July 15, was paraphrased by Hull as follows: "We said it would be unfortunate if any temporary arrangement should be so conceived as to appear to be a departure from the principle adopted by the three Governments at the Moscow Conference definitely rejecting the spheres-of-influence idea. Consequently, this Government hoped that no projected measures would be allowed to prejudice the efforts toward directing the policies of the Allied Governments along lines of collaboration rather than independent action, since any arrangement suggestive of spheres of influence could not but militate against the establishment and effective functioning of a broader system of general security in which all countries would have their part.

"We added that we supposed that the three months' trial period would enable the British and Soviet Governments to determine whether such an arrangement was practicable and efficacious as applying to war conditions only, without in any way affecting the rights and responsibilities which each of the three principal Allied nations would have to exercise during the period of the reestablishment of peace, and afterwards, in regard to the whole of Europe. Finally, we assumed that the arrangement would have neither direct nor indirect validity as affecting the interests of this Government, or

of other Governments associated with the three principal Allies."
Hull *Memoirs*, II, 1458.

22. Churchill, apparently unaware that Hull was dragging his
feet, sent a message to Stalin on July 11 containing the following
paragraph on the Balkan arrangement:

"Some weeks ago it was suggested by Eden to your Ambassador
that the Soviet Government should take the lead in Rumania, and
the British should do the same in Greece. This was only a working arrangement to avoid as much as possible the awful business of
triangular telegrams, which paralyses action. Molotov then suggested
very properly that I should tell the United States, which I did,
and always meant to, and after some discussion the President agreed
to a three-months trial being made. These may be three very important months, Marshal Stalin, July, August, and September. Now
however I see that you find some difficulty in this. I would ask
whether you should not tell us that the plan may be allowed to have
its chance for three months. No one can say it affects the future of
Europe or divides it into spheres. But we can get a clear-headed
policy in each theatre, and we all report to the others what we are
doing. However, if you tell me it is hopeless I shall not take it
amiss." Churchill, *Triumph and Tragedy*, p. 79.

Stalin's reply, dated July 15, read in part as follows: "As regards
the question of Rumania and Greece. . . . One thing is clear to me:
it is that the American Government has some doubts regarding this
question, and that it would be better to revert to this matter when
we receive the American reply to our inquiry. As soon as the observations of the American Government are known, I shall not fail to
write to you further on this question." (Ibid., p. 80.) There is no
evidence of any further written communication from Stalin to
Churchill on this subject.

23. The U. S. reply, in the opinion of one historian, "obviously
deprived the [spheres of responsibility] agreement of much of its
value. If the Americans reserved the right to put a spoke in both the
British and the Russian wheel in any Balkan country, then a division
into operational spheres could have only an insecure foundation."
McNeill, p. 424.

24. Feis, p. 416. "On September 20th, Vishinsky sent Harriman

and Clark Kerr a statement of Soviet plans for the organization of the Allied Control Commission. This provided that the British and American part in the work of the Commission was to be indeed subordinate. Each was to be allowed only five officials on the staff; they were to be permitted to deal with Rumanian officials only through the top officers of the Commission, all of whom were to be Russians; and they were to have to ask permission of the chairman of the Commission before making trips into the country. Vishinsky also claimed that this corresponded with the position of the Soviet members of the staff of the Allied Commission in Italy."

Actually, Russia had broken out of its isolation in Italy by appointing a diplomatic representative there over the objections of the United States and Great Britain; and Vyshinsky now authorized a similar direct but powerless representation in Rumania for the United States and Great Britain, again on the grounds of analogy with Italy. Ibid.

25. McNeill, p. 472.

26. Ibid., p. 390.

27. Ibid., p. 478-79.

28. Vladimir Dedijer, *Tito* (New York: Simon & Schuster, 1953), p. 233.

29. The United States was prepared to give Great Britain a free hand in the Balkans but was not disposed to permit the use of any American troops in that area. Churchill (*Triumph and Tragedy,* p. 208) indicates that there was a division of primary responsibilities as between the United States and Britain in the various operational theatres in Europe. When Churchill became convinced that British intervention in Greece would become necessary, he secured Roosevelt's consent, which was given on the basis that only British troops would be used, although American transport planes were to be made available for the dropping of British parachutists. (Ibid., p. 112.) Throughout the war in the Mediterranean, Churchill pressed for an Allied invasion either at the juncture of Italy with Yugoslavia —the Istrian Peninsula—or along the Yugoslav coast; and throughout the many discussions such plans were rejected by the United States, though usually on military rather than political grounds. The matter was also briefly discussed, in the usual inconclusive manner, at the

Quebec Conference between Roosevelt and Churchill in September 1944.

30. Churchill, *Triumph and Tragedy*, p. 227.

31. Ibid. Churchill's own account here differs from that obtained by the State Department through the American embassies at Moscow and Ankara, which spoke of a 75:25 or 80:20 Russian predominance in Rumania, Bulgaria, and Hungary (Hull *Memoirs,* II, 1458). Although Churchill's 50:50 version of the formula for Hungary must be controlling, it is noteworthy that in interpreting the agreement he clearly intended Russia to have a preponderant role in Hungary, as indicated by the last paragraph quoted under note 32 in this chapter.

32. Churchill, *Triumph and Tragedy*, pp. 227-28. This was the same visit as the one described in Chapter 3 in connection with the Polish issue, when Mikolajczyk was summoned to Moscow to negotiate, but refused to make any concession on the Curzon Line.

Churchill's own interpretation of the Balkans deal with Stalin is contained in a message to his cabinet colleagues which he sent from Moscow on October 12, 1944 (ibid., pp. 233-34):

"The system of percentage is not intended to prescribe the numbers sitting on commissions for the different Balkan countries, but rather to express the interest and sentiment with which the British and Soviet Governments approach the problems of these countries, and so that they might reveal their minds to each other in some way that could be comprehended. It is not intended to be more than a guide, and of course in no way commits the United States, nor does it attempt to set up a rigid system of spheres of interest. It may however help the United States to see how their two principal Allies feel about these regions when the picture is presented as a whole.

"Thus it is seen that quite naturally Soviet Russia has vital interests in the countries bordering on the Black Sea, by one of whom, Rumania, she has been most wantonly attacked with twenty-six divisions, and with the other of whom, Bulgaria, she has ancient ties. Great Britain feels it right to show particular respect to Russian views about these two countries, and to the Soviet desire to take the lead in a practical way in guiding them in the name of the common cause.

145

"Similarly Great Britain has a long tradition of friendship with Greece, and a direct interest as a Mediterranean Power in her future. In this war Great Britain lost 30,000 men in trying to resist the German-Italian invasion of Greece, and wishes to play a leading part in guiding Greece out of her present troubles, maintaining that close agreement with the United States which has hitherto characterised Anglo-American policy in this quarter. Here it is understood that Great Britain will take the lead in a military sense and try to help the existing Royal Greek Government to establish itself in Athens upon as broad and united a basis as possible. Soviet Russia would be ready to concede this position and function to Great Britain in the same sort of way as Britain would recognise the intimate relationship between Russia and Rumania. This would prevent in Greece the growth of hostile factions waging civil war upon each other and involving the British and Russian Governments in vexatious arguments and conflict of policy.

"Coming to the case of Yugoslavia, the numerical symbol 50:50 is intended to be the foundation of joint action and an agreed policy between the two powers now closely involved, so as to favour the creation of a united Yugoslavia after all elements there have been joined together to the utmost in driving out the Nazi invaders. It is intended to prevent, for instance, armed strife between Croats and Slovenes on the one side and powerful and numerous elements in Serbia on the other, and also to produce a joint and friendly policy towards Marshal Tito, while ensuring that weapons furnished to him are used against the common Nazi foe rather than for internal purposes. Such a policy, pursued in common by Britain and Soviet Russia, without any thought of special advantages to themselves, would be of real benefit.

"As it is the Soviet armies which are obtaining control of Hungary, it would be natural that a major share of influence should rest with them, subject of course to agreement with Great Britain and probably the United States, who, though not actually operating in Hungary, must view it as a Central European and not a Balkan State."

33. Robert E. Sherwood, *Roosevelt and Hopkins* (New York: Harper, 1948), pp. 833-34; *Stalin Correspondence*, II, 162. Stalin replied: "I was somewhat puzzled by your message of October 5. I

had imagined that Mr. Churchill was coming to Moscow in keeping with an agreement reached with you at Quebec. It appears, however, that my supposition is at variance with reality." Ibid., II, 163.

34. Sherwood, p. 834.

35. Feis, p. 450.

36. Ibid., p. 451.

37. McNeill (p. 496) says "Stalin showed no hesitation in agreeing that the operation would be desirable." Feis (p. 445) says Stalin "encouraged" the idea of a British landing on the Istrian Peninsula "and thence across Northwest Yugoslavia and through the Alps; and on to Vienna, there to join up with Soviet forces coming from the east." Feis's account continues:

"Then during the formal military discussion on the 14th, Stalin and General Antonov repeated the suggestion. In accordance with the agreement which Stalin had reached with Tito Russian troops in Yugoslavia were not going to advance farther west than Belgrade; they were going to leave it to Tito's forces to clear the Germans out of the rest of the country. Stalin said he would be glad to see the British move north from Istria, go through the mountains, and join the Soviet columns which would be, he hoped, coming west from Hungary in the neighborhood of Vienna."

38. *Yalta Papers* (see chap. 1, note 1), pp. 494, 545.

39. Dedijer (p. 234) reports that during his talk with Stalin in late September, Tito had said that if the British landed in Yugoslavia, "we should offer determined resistance." Stalin had not replied. "Obviously this answer was not to his liking. Was he at the moment pondering over the arrangements he had made for a division of spheres of influence?"

Feis (p. 445) comments: "It is impossible to resist conjecture why, at this time, and for the first time, Stalin favored such a strategy. Was it only because he wanted this threat at the flank or rear of the German lines in the south, to be sure that they would not be able to shift forces to his central front or Hungary, where it was becoming apparent that the Germans were going to contest every mile? Or was he also displaying his sincere intention to conform to the chart of 'spheres of responsibility' which he and Churchill had marked out a few nights before. . . ? Or was he trying to embroil the British in a clash with Tito, who he knew had grown opposed to having them land in Yugoslavia?"

Wilmot offers another explanation. He says that in the autumn of 1944 the Soviet High Command "was extremely doubtful of its ability to continue the offensive through Poland. It was so concerned on this account that, when Churchill was in Moscow in October, Stalin had strongly advocated that the Allied Armies in Italy should cross the Adriatic and drive north through Yugoslavia in the direction of Vienna. Since Stalin had previously opposed every plan for Allied ground operations in the Balkans, this proposal can only have been dictated by the belief that the intervention of Anglo-American forces in Yugoslavia would tie down the German divisions which were being withdrawn from the Southern Balkans to Hungary, and might even attract reserves from Poland. Stalin would hardly have suggested this move unless he had believed that it would expedite his own advance to Vienna and Berlin." Chester Wilmot, *The Struggle for Europe* (London: Collins, 1952), p. 630.

40. McNeill, p. 496n. Cf. also note 29 to this chapter.

41. Churchill, *Triumph and Tragedy,* p. 289.

42. Ibid.

43. Ibid.

44. The Stettinius statement, dated December 5—the day when the insurrection broke out in Greece—was worded as follows: "The position of this Government has been consistently that the composition of the Italian Government is purely an Italian affair except in the case of appointments where important military factors are concerned. This Government has not in any way intimated to the Italian Government that there would be any opposition on its part to Count Sforza. Since Italy is an area of combined responsibility, we have reaffirmed to both the British and Italian Governments that we expect the Italians to work out their problems of government along democratic lines without influence from outside. This policy would apply to an even more pronounced degree with regard to governments of the United Nations in their liberated territories." Leland M. Goodrich and Marie J. Carroll, eds., *Documents on American Foreign Relations, 1944-1945* (Princeton, N. J.: Princeton University Press, 1947), II, 172. The last sentence clearly applied to Greece, and it especially rankled with Churchill.

45. Churchill, *Triumph and Tragedy*, pp. 298-99.

46. "When we recall what had happened to Poland, to Hungary, and Czechoslovakia in these later years," Churchill later wrote, "we may be grateful to Fortune for giving us at this critical moment the calm, united strength of determined leaders of all parties. . . . There was a strong current of vague opinion, and even passion. . . . Here again any Government which had rested on a less solid foundation than the National Coalition might well have been shaken to pieces." Ibid., p. 293.

With respect to the merits of his action, the former Prime Minister could not repress a feeling of satisfaction that they were subsequently acknowledged: "Now that the free world has learnt so much more than was then understood about the Communist movement in Greece and elsewhere, many readers will be astonished at the vehement attacks to which His Majesty's Government, and I in particular at its head, were subjected. The vast majority of the American press violently condemned our action, which they declared falsified the cause for which they had gone to war. If the editors of all these well-meaning organs will look back at what they wrote then and compare it with what they think now they will, I am sure, be surprised." Ibid., p. 292.

47. Ibid., p. 293.

48. *Yalta Papers*, p. 781.

49. Ibid., p. 849.

50. Ibid., p. 154.

51. The British position paper at Yalta made a distinction in this respect between Bulgaria and Hungary on the one hand, and Rumania on the other. *Yalta Papers*, p. 513-514. The American position paper, on the other hand, lumped Rumania, Bulgaria, and Hungary together. Ibid., p. 568.

52. Churchill, *Triumph and Tragedy*, p. 348.

53. *Yalta Papers*, p. 781.

54. Churchill, *Triumph and Tragedy*, p. 353.

55. *Yalta Papers*, p. 617.

56. *Stalin Correspondence*, I, 340. Churchill used this rather renunciatory statement as an introduction to his categorical rejection of "the Yugoslav model" as a precedent for Poland where in his view a much clearer agreement existed.

149

Beginnings of the Cold War

It is noteworthy that Churchill refers to his spheres-of-influence deal with Stalin in a letter dated April 28, 1945—in other words, two months after the Yalta Conference—as though it were still supposed to be in effect.

57. Feis, p. 628.

58. Royal Institute of International Affairs, *The Soviet-Yugoslav Dispute* (London, 1948), letter from the Central Committee of Communist Party of Soviet Union to Central Committee of Communist Party of Yugoslavia, dated May 4, 1948:

"In this respect, the speech by Comrade Tito in Ljubljana in May 1945 is very characteristic. He said: 'It is said that this war is a just war and we have considered it as such. However, we seek also a just end; we demand that every one shall be master in his own house; we do not want to pay for others; we do not want to be used as a bribe in international bargaining; we do not want to get involved in any policy of spheres of interest.' This was said in connection with the question of Trieste. As is well known, after a series of territorial concessions for the benefit of Yugoslavia, which the Soviet Union extracted from the Anglo-Americans, the latter, together with the French, rejected the Soviet proposal to hand Trieste over to Yugoslavia and occupied Trieste with their own forces, which were then in Italy. Since all other means were exhausted, the Soviet Union had only one other method left for gaining Trieste for Yugoslavia—to start war with the Anglo-Americans over Trieste and take it by force. The Yugoslav comrades could not fail to realize that after such a hard war the USSR could not enter another."

59. Churchill, *Triumph and Tragedy*, p. 560.

This was the second reference by Churchill to the spheres-of-influence deal (cf. note 56) after the Yalta Conference, where it was supposed to have been superseded, at least in the American view, by the Declaration of Liberated Europe. Cf. also chap. 7, Question 56.

60. Historians have been puzzled by the presence of a few anti-Communists in the Groza government that was installed through Russian intervention. "One of them, Gheorghe Tatarescu, had as Prime Minister in 1936 sentenced Anna Pauker, a leading Communist, to jail. Their inclusion can best be explained as a pious gesture to honour the . . . percentage figure which Stalin and Churchill had fixed in October in Moscow." McNeill, p. 575n.

A specialist on Rumanian affairs wrote in 1951: "Certain events in 1945 are rather difficult to explain on the premises of a fixed intention to sovietize eastern Europe. Why was Hungary permitted to have free elections in 1945, elections which brought in an anti-Communist majority? Even in Rumania, the Soviet presentation to King Michael of its highest award, the Order of Victory, would seem an unnecessarily extravagant gesture if he was to be dethroned at an early date. The inclusion in the Groza Government of such a questionable person as Tatarescu, who was not really needed for his technical competence, whom the local Rumanian Communists regarded with great distaste, and whose presence certainly did not greatly reassure business circles, is perhaps best, if rather weirdly, explained by the Soviet determination to have a 'bourgeois' politician in the new coalition." Henry L. Roberts, *Rumania* (New Haven: Yale University Press, 1951), p. 271.

61. Feis, p. 452.

62. Royal Institute of International Affairs, *The Realignment of Europe,* edited by Arnold Toynbee (London: Oxford University Press, 1955), p. 318.

63. Ibid., pp. 320-21.

64. Ibid., p. 322. The November 4, 1945 election is termed "probably the freest general election ever held in the history of Hungary." That the outcome was not an accident is suggested by the fact that contrary to obvious Soviet expectations, equally free elections in Budapest during the summer of 1945 had yielded a Smallholder majority; and that anti-Communist agrarian party was known to be stronger in the countryside than in the capital.

65. *Documents on American Foreign Relations, 1943-1944* (Boston: World Peace Foundation, 1945), pp. 642-44.

66. The Communists had minority representations in coalition governments at that time in France, Italy, Belgium, Luxembourg, Norway, and Denmark. In all of those countries the Communists were later evicted from the government when they resorted to subversion and violence.

67. *The Realignment of Europe,* p. 333.

68. *Stalin Correspondence,* II, 202.

69. Ibid., II, 239.

70. Ibid., II, 242.

71. *Potsdam Papers* (see chap. 2, note 1), I, 258-59.

72. Ibid., II, 644.

73. Churchill, *Triumph and Tragedy*, p. 636.

74. *Potsdam Papers*, II, 1044.

75. Ibid., II, 150-51.

76. Byrnes, p. 73.

77. Philip E. Mosely, *Face to Face with Russia* (New York: Foreign Policy Association "Headline Series" No. 70, 1948), p. 23. Also, *The Kremlin in World Politics* (New York: Vintage Books, 1960), p. 214.

78. *Potsdam Papers*, II, 525.

6

Gifts, Loans, and Disappointments

On January 3, 1945 Foreign Minister Molotov handed Ambassador Harriman an *aide-mémoire* proposing that the United States grant Russia a $6,000,000,000 credit for postwar reconstruction, at 2¼ per cent interest.[1] Our ambassador commented:

> Molotov made it very plain that the Soviet Government placed high importance on a large postwar credit as a basis for the development of "Soviet-American relations." . . . It is, of course, my very strong and earnest opinion that the question of the credit should be tied into our overall diplomatic relations with the Soviet Union and at the appropriate time the Russians should be given to understand that our willingness to cooperate wholeheartedly with them in their vast reconstruction problems will depend upon their behavior in international matters. I feel, too, that the eventual Lend-Lease settlement should also be borne in mind in this connection.[2]

The ambassador thought that the matter of a postwar credit was likely to come up at the next high-level meeting between

Roosevelt and Stalin.[3] However, it was not raised by the Russians at Yalta; nor did the United States use the Russian eagerness for aid to improve its bargaining position at the Crimea Conference.[4]

The published documentation on this aspect of American-Soviet relations during the closing phase of the war is still incomplete. But some indications can be gleaned from sources now publicly available, notably from the Yalta Papers. In that volume there is, for instance, a memorandum from President Roosevelt to the Secretary of State which contains this interesting passage in connection with the problem of the postwar treatment of German industry: "In regard to the Soviet government, it is true that we have no idea as yet what they have in mind, but we have to remember that in their occupied territory they will do more or less what they wish. We cannot afford to get into a position of merely recording protests on our part unless there is some chance of some of the protests being heeded. I do not intend by this to break off or delay negotiations with the Soviet government over lend-lease either on the contract basis or on the proposed Fourth Protocol basis. . . ."[5] The question of what happened to the Soviet application for a credit is indeed so interlocked with the record of the last phase of Lend-Lease and notably with the so-called Fourth Protocol, and also with the question of German reparations, that that background must first be summarized.

Hitler launched the German invasion of the Soviet Union on June 21, 1941. One month later, on July 21, President Roosevelt ordered "immediate and substantial shipments of assistance to the Union of Soviet Socialist Republics." These initial shipments were not gifts but were financed by "advances" from the U.S. Treasury against future Soviet deliveries of gold and strategic materials. In September, the Russian ambassador to the United

States initiated negotiations for military assistance on a repayable credit basis. During the same month, after Hopkins had conferred with Stalin in Moscow and had reported his conviction that Russia would be able to offer prolonged resistance to the invader, a joint British-American mission under Lord Beaverbrook and Ambassador Harriman was dispatched to Moscow to discuss a large military aid program. Meanwhile, President Roosevelt, mindful of possible Catholic opposition to American aid to the Soviet Union, had dispatched Myron C. Taylor, his special ambassador to Pope Pius XII, to Rome to obtain Vatican support for such an aid program.

Myron Taylor's mission to Rome, as reported by Robert Sherwood, was completed at the time when Harriman's mission to Moscow was starting. Taylor "made a supremely tactful and legitimate presentation of the President's case at the Vatican, where he met with a most sympathetic reception. While the results of this mission were given no great amount of publicity, they were reflected in the attitude of the Catholic hierarchy in the United States and no serious issue was raised"[6] when Russia in November 1941 was declared eligible for Lend-Lease assistance. Even so, however, the terms offered by Roosevelt to Stalin on October 30—which the Soviet dictator immediately accepted —did not yet involve the full Lend-Lease treatment. They provided for supplies up to $1 billion in value, to be repaid without interest over a period of ten years starting five years after the war. No such explicit arrangements for repayment of Lend-Lease had been made with Great Britain or other recipients.

Another important difference between Lend-Lease aid to Russia and Lend-Lease to Great Britain lay in the manner in which the items and quantities were determined. In the case of Britain, the United States received and discussed with its ally all information relevant to particular requests such as Britain's own productive capacity, inventories, and the use to which the items were to be put. This resulted in a close intertwining of the American and British economies, paralleling the joint U. S.-British formulation of war plans. No such relationship existed with Russia, which throughout the war regarded its Western allies with utmost suspicion. Were they not, according to the Communist view of the world, basically hostile, capitalist states just like Hitler's Germany? Had they not, in the Communist perspective, tried to direct Nazi expansionism to the East, and did they not hope that Germany and Russia would mutually exhaust each other so that the West could emerge victorious without suffering terrible losses such as Russia was enduring?

To the Russians, the acid test of Western intentions was the establishment of a second front on the continent, and Stalin did not cease to clamor for such a landing that would divert a substantial number of German divisions from the eastern front. As is known, Roosevelt authorized Molotov in May 1942 to inform Stalin that he "expected" that a second front would be created that very year;[7] Churchill persuaded the President to substitute a landing in North Africa for a contemplated diversionary action in France;[8] and Stalin subsequently claimed most vehemently that he had been deceived.[9] (This disagreement became accentuated when the planned major cross-Channel invasion was postponed from 1943 to 1944.) Throughout the war Stalin suspected, or pretended to suspect, that the Western Allies were about to make a separate peace with Germany; and on more than one occasion, especially in 1942, the Western Allies suspected that Russian resistance to the German onslaught might collapse completely—and had not Stalin made a sudden and unexpected deal with Hitler once before?

In any event, the programming of Lend-Lease for Russia was devoid of any of the spirit of cordiality and comradeship which

Gifts, Loans, and Disappointments

characterized the aid discussions between the United States and Great Britain. The Russians would state their requirements but refuse to explain them or to give any information on the use to which the particular items would be put or what their own production of them was; they rigidly insisted on their own specifications even when this entailed delays and extra costs that must have been harmful to their own purposes; and they refused to permit the kind of inspection of end-item use that was customary as well as helpful elsewhere. Intelligent planning of priorities and assistance in the most efficient use of the material furnished were thus made impossible. General Deane, the head of the wartime U. S. Military Mission to the U. S. S. R., has testified vividly in his book, *Strange Alliance,* to the shortsightedness of the Soviet policy of secretiveness, which prevented American assistance from being as useful as it might have been.[10] At the same time, he attributed Russian failure to substantiate requests to the absence of records comparable to those in use by the Western Allies.[11]

By the middle of 1942, aid to Russia was placed on the same basis as aid to Great Britain in so far as the absence of any quantitative limitation or specific provision for repayment was concerned. The so-called Master Agreement with the Soviet Union stated that the President, pursuant to the Act of Congress of March 11, 1941, had determined the defense of the Soviet Union to be "vital to the defense of the United States" and that the determination of final terms and conditions of extending such aid should be deferred until later. In the preamble, the two governments also declared that they were cooperating in "laying the basis of a just and enduring world peace securing order under law" and referred to their allegiance to the principles embodied in the Atlantic Charter. Under Article III the Soviet government promised not to transfer Lend-Lease mate-

157

rials to other countries, and under Article VII the Soviets, like other recipients, subscribed to American trade policies, notably "the elimination of all forms of discriminatory treatment in international commerce, and . . . the reduction of tariffs and other trade barriers."[12]

This was the framework, but the actual items and quantities to be shipped were determined on an annual basis in the form of the so-called Supply Protocols, which also involved Great Britain and later Canada. The first such protocol had already been negotiated by Beaverbrook and Harriman in 1941. The second protocol was negotiated in 1942, and the third covered the period from mid-1943 to mid-1944. These negotiations were usually prolonged and sometimes acrimonious, but the needs of the eastern front were so urgent that Russia enjoyed an almost absolute priority even while the various Protocols were still under negotiation. (When Molotov was in Washington in May 1942 it was made clear to him that the strain on Allied shipping which this involved had inevitable repercussions on preparations for the second front.[13])

Several reasons have been adduced for the preferential treatment which Russia came to enjoy in the matter of Lend-Lease. First, there is the fact that Russia up to 1944 bore the brunt of the fight against Nazi Germany, suffering enormous losses in men, material, and productive power[14] at a time when the United States was husbanding its manpower and vastly increasing its own productive capacity. Second, the inability of the Western Allies to open a major second front, despite what the Russians could consider commitments to that effect, inevitably placed both the United States and Britain under some moral obligation to give maximum assistance at least in the material field. Thirdly, up to the turning point at Stalingrad in 1943 there was a real and perhaps justified fear that Russia might leave the war. Then later, as we have seen (Chapter 3), there was the need for coordination with the Russian offensives after the cross-Channel invasion was launched. Finally, as stated in Chapter 1, it was felt that Russian military assistance would be required in the Far East even after the defeat of Germany. The basic premise of all aid to Russia was, of course, that it made our own job of defeating the common enemy that much easier. As President Truman has stated: "Every soldier of Russia, England and Australia who had been equipped by Lend-Lease . . . reduced by that much the dangers that faced our young men in winning [the war]. We may never get the money back, but the lives we saved are right here in America."[15]

Total Lend-Lease shipments to the Soviet Union up to September 1945 amounted to $9.5 billion, or 29 per cent of shipments to all countries. In addition to bulk items such as explosives, petroleum products, food and steel, the shipments included 14,700 planes, 7,000 tanks, 52,000 jeeps, 376,000 trucks, 35,000 motorcycles, 2,000 locomotives, 11,000 freight cars, 3,800,000 tires, and over 15 million army boots—all of which clearly contributed to the fighting power and especially the mobility of the Russian armies.[16] According to one authority, American Lend-Lease trucks represented between 10 and 15 per cent of the trucks used on the entire Soviet front.[17] As General Deane has written, "At the Teheran Conference, Stalin told the President and the Prime Minister that his margin of superiority over the Germans was about sixty divisions which could be shifted rapidly from place to place on their extended front in order to provide massed power for a breakthrough in areas of their own choice. It is impossible to conceive how these divisions could have been moved rapidly, or even at all, had they not had American trucks to ride in, American shoes to march in, and American food to sustain them."[18] While this statement is perhaps somewhat exaggerated[19] and tends to overlook the improvement of Russia's own war production by the end of 1943, qualified observers agree that Lend-Lease may well have saved the Russian front from collapse during the early part of the war and obviously contributed appreciably to the later decisive Russian victories on the eastern front.

Approximately one-third of Lend-Lease exports to the U. S. S. R. consisted of industrial materials and products for the expansion and relocation of Soviet industry. Thus the United States furnished a half billion dollars' worth of machine tools as well as electrical furnaces and generators. In addition, entire factories, including a tire plant, aluminum rolling mill, pipe fabricating mills, and petroleum refining equipment were exported to assist the U. S. S. R. in expanding its war production.[20] This was clearly in the American interest as long as the Russian armies were hard pressed and even later when they had started to strike their mortal blows against the retreating Germans. However, when the time came to discuss the Fourth Russian Supply Protocol, covering the fiscal year beginning July 1, 1944, it was found that the proportion of Russian requests for industrial equipment and machinery had gone up sharply, amounting to more than $1 billion in value.[21] The question arose whether such items could be delivered before the end of the war and whether, indeed, they were intended to assist Russia in prosecuting the war or were intended for postwar reconstruction. There was strong sentiment in Congress, where the extension of the Lend-Lease Act was by no means assured,[22] that this instrument of wartime assistance must not be used for the purposes of postwar reconstruction. (In April 1945, when the Act came up for its last Congressional renewal, such a limitation was actually written into the law.)

Accordingly, the United States proposed in May 1944 to conclude a supplementary agreement to the Fourth Protocol providing that any items that would be principally used for postwar reconstruction should be bought by the Russians on credit, at the rate of 2⅜ per cent and repayable over a period of 25 to 30 years. But the Russians insisted on a rate of 2 per cent, and after prolonged haggling the matter remained in deadlock.[23] Apparently, the Russians calculated that at the end of the war in Europe the United States would find its economy underemployed and that pressure from industry and labor, particularly in factories that stood to gain from pending exports to Russia, would compel the U. S. government to extend credit on more favorable terms.[24] The absence of agreement on the interest rate delayed conclusion of the Fourth Protocol until April 17, 1945. Even then, however, the question of post-Lend-Lease shipments was left in suspense. The Fourth Protocol simply declared that items ineligible for Lend-Lease "may be purchased by the U. S. S. R. if it so elects,"[25] leaving the matter of credits and interest for further discussion. By that time, of course, the Russian request for a $6 billion credit at 2¼ per cent interest had been left unanswered for three and a half months.

Why did the United States government insist on concluding a supplementary Lend-Lease agreement with the Soviet Union to provide for payment of interest at the rate of 2⅜ per cent on postwar shipments when it was confronted with a Russian request for a larger credit at the rate of 2¼ per cent? Should not the matter of interest have been negotiable? One answer, certainly, is that new Congressional authority was needed for the credit, whereas the pending orders could have been accommodated under authority of Article 3 (c) of the Lend-Lease Act. It also appears, however, that it had become a matter of principle for the American negotiators that the terms of 2⅜ per cent, which had been declared to be "final," must not be modified.

When the Treasury Department, for instance, proposed that

the whole business of interest on industrial shipments under Lend-Lease be simply dropped, Assistant Secretary Clayton wrote to Secretary Stettinius: "We told the Soviet negotiators, in full good faith and with definite Treasury concurrence, that the last 3 (c) proposals [for a supplementary agreement] we made to them were our final offer, and that because of legal and other grounds, we could not grant them any better terms. If we should now make the proposals except for the exclusion of interest charges we could not help but give the impression to the Soviet authorities that what we said last summer was not true, and thus we might unwittingly kindle the fire of suspicion which they have had in the past as to our good faith."[26] The idea that an advantageous economic offer to the Soviet Union, at a time when that country was most anxious to secure help for its postwar reconstruction, might "kindle the fires of suspicion" seems strange in retrospect, but it was apparently held with sincerity and certainly with great tenacity by the U. S. negotiators.

Another reason adduced by Assistant Secretary Clayton in the same document related to the U. S. bargaining position on other matters: "By making this new proposal [to waive interest on shipments of industrial goods ordered under Lend-Lease but which were not for war purposes] we would definitely give the impression that we were most anxious, on almost any terms, to make available postwar goods to the Soviet Union. While we are naturally desirous to increase our trade with the Soviet Union to the maximum, and it is in our interest to do so, it would be tactically harmful to deepen the impression they already have that no matter what happens we are going to have to sell goods to the Soviet Union in order to keep our economy going."[27] The Clayton memorandum was written on January 20, 1945, two weeks before the Yalta Conference, where the United

States held a rather weak hand with respect to the issues involving Poland and the countries of southeastern Europe.

President Roosevelt's briefing book for the Yalta Conference included a paper on the "Russian Request for Financing of Acquisitions of Capital Equipment During and After the War" which discussed both the $6 billion credit request and the question of further industrial equipment under Lend-Lease. On the latter subject, the paper told the President that "the Department [of State] proposes to inform the Soviets through Ambassador Harriman that no long-range industrial equipment can be put into production until agreement be reached on the terms of the Lend-Lease 3-C agreement which has been under discussion since May 1944." With respect to the credit request, it was stated that "the Department believes the U. S. S. R. will contract only such credits as it can service. Current Russian gold production of about $200 million a year could service a $6 billion credit on the terms proposed by the Soviets; [or] about $3 billion on usual Export-Import Bank credits." The paper ended with the simple observation: "Postwar credits to the U. S. S. R. can serve as a useful instrument in our overall relations with the U. S. S. R."[28] In a telegram to Harriman a week before Yalta, the State Department reported to him that "the general matter of credits to Russia has been discussed with the President who has displayed a keen interest and believes that it should not be pressed further pending actual discussions between himself and Marshal Stalin and other Soviet officials."[29] However, the matter did not come up between Roosevelt and Stalin in any of their discussions.

The question of credits for Russian reconstruction was not unrelated to the problem of German reparations. Stalin insisted on such reparations at Yalta not only as a matter of just retribution but also to help bind up the terrible wounds that Russia had suffered at the hands of the Nazi invaders. He proposed that the total amount—to be paid in the form of industrial equipment, current production, and forced labor—be fixed at $20 billion, with half of it to go to the Soviet Union. Roosevelt did not oppose this proposal, although he was worried that excessive reparations would result in Germany becoming a burden on the world, and thus on the United States.[30] Churchill, on the other hand, was directly opposed to the fixing of such large reparations, as he foresaw that a starving Germany could become politically unmanageable and that, if Russia took out vast reparations, it might turn out that the West would have to put in compensating aid to the Germans. "The Prime Minister concluded," according to the Bohlen minutes, "that if you wished a horse to pull a wagon you would at least have to give it fodder."[31] Clearly, the question of reparations went to the heart of the kind of Germany there would be after the war, and whether there would be one occupied Germany or separate states in which each occupying power would do what it pleased.

This problem had been foreseen by American diplomats, who had tried to work out a policy for the postwar treatment of Germany in 1944. As reported by one of his former staff members, John G. Winant, the American Ambassador in London, had pointed out to Washington

> that the Russian need for material aid in repairing the vast destruction in the Soviet Union was bound to make the Soviet Government particularly eager to receive reparations deliveries from Germany on a large scale. Since the major part of German industry was located in the western zones, the Allies must try to work out, in advance, a reparations policy which would satisfy a part of the Soviet demands without involving an undue burden for the United

States. . . . He urged that the United States consider ways of helping the recovery of the Soviet economy, such assistance to be linked to the achievement of a satisfactory settlement of the problem of German reparations and of the most important political issues between the two governments.[32]

Winant's pleas, however, were ignored and as a result the United States at the time of Yalta had no clear policy either on reparations or on the question of postwar assistance to the Soviet Union.

In the United States Senate, the question of the $6 billion credit to the Soviet Union came up incidentally when the extension of the Lend-Lease Act was under discussion in the Foreign Relations Committee on March 28, 1945. Foreign Economic Administrator Leo T. Crowley explained the contemplated procedures pursuant to Article 3 (c) of the Lend-Lease Act for "orderly and efficient liquidation of war-supply contracts . . . through the purchase by foreign governments for cash or on credit, of such supplies as may not be produced or delivered in time to be of use in the war." Senator Wiley thereupon asked for elucidation of newspaper reports about a $6 billion credit to Russia under Lend-Lease. Oscar Cox, the deputy administrator, acknowledged that a request for such a credit had been received but said that the Russians had been told it could not be handled under Lend-Lease. Senator Vandenberg next inquired whether the Russians had asked for any Lend-Lease commitments for the period after July 1, 1945 and Cox replied that they had been asked to submit requests for a Fifth Protocol. "Do you expect [such a request]?" Senator Vandenberg asked. "Well," Cox replied, "that depends on what happens in Germany and what the Soviets do in the Japanese war." To which Senator

Vandenberg, who did not seem adverse to some bargaining, replied: "I hope it depends a lot on what happens at San Francisco, too."[33]

By the time the war in Europe ended, in May 1945, the situation with regard to Lend-Lease, reparations, and credits for Russia was as follows. As we have seen, a Fourth Lend-Lease Protocol, confined strictly to war-necessary items, had been signed in April, leaving in suspense the question of items in the "pipeline" which Russia would have to purchase, with the matter of interest rates still in deadlock. The size of reparations to be paid by Germany had not been settled by the Yalta Conference but had been referred to an inter-Allied commission set up in Moscow.[34] That Commission had produced no agreement —in fact, it produced angry acrimony. The Russians claimed that they had been let down by the United States because Roosevelt at Yalta had agreed to the $20 billion figure "as a basis of discussion" whereas the American representatives in Moscow sided with the British in favor of lesser amounts.[35] As for the Russian request for a $6 billion credit, available evidence suggests that the question became tangled up in a legal argument in Washington whether the Export-Import Bank could extend a loan to Russia as long as the Soviet government repudiated the debts contracted in the United States by the Kerensky government during World War I.[36]

Clearly, the United States had lost interest in the idea of a credit for Russian reconstruction in view of all the disagreements with Russia that had arisen since Yalta. The Forrestal Diaries include a message from Ambassador Harriman dated April 11, 1945, in which he had questioned the desirability of giving preferential treatment to Russia in postwar trade and had stated: "Our experience has incontrovertibly proved that it is not possible to bank general good will in Moscow, and I agree

with the Department that we should retain current control of
these credits in order to be in a position to protect American
vital interests in the formulative period immediately following
the war."[37] This was one day before the death of President
Roosevelt. As we have seen (Chapter 4), when Truman had his
angry interview with Molotov with regard to Poland less than
two weeks later, the new President only hinted that Russia
could expect no postwar assistance from the United States if it
did not satisfy American public and Congressional opinion. As
far as can be determined from published records, the United
States did not make any proposals or counterproposals to the
Russian request for a credit until the matter was revived in a
different form in 1946 after another Russian request for a loan
(made in August 1945) was discovered, having been lost for
six months.[38]

As soon as the war in Europe was over, the United States
government cut off all Lend-Lease shipments and even ordered
some ships en route to Russia and other European nations to
turn around and return to American ports for unloading. This
produced an outcry, especially from Great Britain, which had
been led to believe that Lend-Lease shipments would continue
at a rate of approximately $2¼ billion after V-E Day.[39] In
Russia, as we have seen from Stalin's complaint to Hopkins
(Chapter 2), it was regarded as a hostile blow to bend the
Soviet government to the American will on other issues. However, the sudden cessation of Lend-Lease aid was technically in
keeping with the letter of the Lend-Lease Act, which, as
amended in April 1945, precluded any shipments for postwar
relief, rehabilitation, or reconstruction. On the other hand, as
Great Britain was still in the war against Japan and as Russia
had undertaken to join that war within three months of the end
of the war in Europe, the abrupt cessation was unnecessary and,

as recognized by President Truman himself, unwise; and he rescinded the order.

President Truman has written frankly about this episode that it taught him a lesson early in his administration—"that I must always know what is in the document I sign. . . . If I had read the order, as I should have, the incident would not have occurred."[40] The document had been submitted to him by the Foreign Economic Administrator and the Acting Secretary of State and he had been under the impression, Truman wrote, that it involved reduction, but not cessation, of American aid. However, the manner in which the order was executed was unfortunate.

> The sudden stoppage of Lend-Lease [Truman wrote] was clearly a case of policy-making on the part of Crowley and Grew. It was perfectly proper and right, of course, to plan for the eventual cutting off of Lend-Lease to Russia and other countries, but it should have been done on a gradual basis which would not have made it appear as if somebody had been deliberately snubbed. After all, we had extracted an agreement from the Russians at Yalta that they would be in the Japanese war three months after the Germans folded up. We were eager for the Russians to get into the war with Japan. . . . With this situation in mind, I clarified the government's attitude.[41]

In a press and radio conference on May 23, the President declared that the order behind Crowley's action was intended to be not a cancellation of shipments but a gradual readjustment to conditions following the collapse of Germany. He also made it clear that all allocations provided for by treaty or protocol would be delivered and that every American commitment would be fulfilled.

This is what Hopkins explained to Stalin in their conversation in Moscow on May 27, 1945. Neither the question of a credit nor the disposition of pending shipments under the abortive 3(c) agreement were discussed on that occasion. The latter subject was subsequently negotiated between the U. S. and Soviet governments and an agreement ("Disposition of Lend-Lease Supplies in Inventory or Procurement in the United States") was concluded in the fall of 1945, providing that "interest on the unpaid balance of the total amount . . . shall be paid by the Government of the Union of Soviet Socialist Republics at a fixed rate of 2⅜ percent per annum"[42]—the rate on which the United States had insisted for one and one-half years. However, three-quarters of the approximately $1 billion in postwar orders which the Russians had tried to include in the Lend-Lease program had never been put into production. As one historian put it: trying to drive a shrewd bargain, the Russians had overreached themselves.[43] At the same time, while America's economic power played such an important role in the wartime military relations with the Soviet Union, it played no role at all in the attempts to work out with Russia a viable and honorable peace.

NOTES

1. *Yalta Papers* (see chap. 1, note 1), pp. 310-11. The Soviet request was couched in terms that made it appear to conform to American as well as Russian wishes: "Having in mind the repeated statements of American public figures concerning the desirability of receiving extensive large Soviet orders for the postwar and transition period, the Soviet Government considers it possible to place orders on the basis of long term credits to the amount of six billion

dollars. Such orders would be for manufactured goods (oil pipes, rails, railroad cars, locomotives and other products) and industrial equipment. . . . The United States Government should grant to the Soviet Union a discount of 20% off the government contracts with firms, of all orders placed before the end of the war and falling under this credit. Prices for orders placed after the end of the war should be left to agreement between the American firms in question and Soviet representatives."

2. Ibid., p. 313. To Molotov, Harriman said, "speaking entirely personally, that I thought the moment entirely favorable for arriving at a final agreement about the Lend Lease orders for the war period and for the opening of preliminary discussions on the question of credits after the war." (Ibid., p. 311.)

3. Ibid.

4. There was one casual reference to the loan request at the luncheon meeting of Foreign Ministers at Yalta on February 5, 1945. According to the Page Minutes (ibid., p. 610), "Mr. Molotov indicated that the Soviet Government expected to receive reparations from Germany in kind and hoped that the United States would furnish the Soviet Union with long term credits. Mr. Stettinius stated that his Government had studied this question and that he personally was ready to discuss it at any time with Mr. Molotov." The matter was not brought up again by either side.

5. Ibid., p. 155. The memorandum was dated September 29, 1944, or three months prior to the Russian loan application. It related, of course, not to the question of offering credits to the Russians but rather to the need for a policy on German industry which would have some appeal to the Russians. The reference to Lend-Lease, however, can be taken as an indication that Roosevelt felt that a punitive policy would be as unlikely to achieve results as "a position of merely recording protests." Secretary of the Treasury Morgenthau in a memorandum to President Roosevelt dated January 1, 1945, or three days before news of the Russian loan application was received, recommended "a plan for comprehensive aid to Russia during her reconstruction period." He said that Harriman had expressed great interest and would like to see the plan advanced. He stated, "I am convinced that if we were to come forward now and present to the

Russians a concrete plan to aid them in the reconstruction period it would contribute a great deal towards ironing out many of the difficulties we have been having with respect to their problems and policies." (Ibid., pp. 309-10.) Morgenthau envisaged credits in the amount of $10 billion (ibid., p. 315.)

6. Robert E. Sherwood, *Roosevelt and Hopkins* (New York: Harper, 1948), pp. 384 and 398.

7. Ibid., p. 563.

8. Churchill was considerably less categorical in giving assurances regarding a cross-Channel invasion in 1942. Churchill, *The Hinge of Fate* (see chap. 3, note 5), p. 342. For his arguments against an invasion of the Continent in 1942, which he advanced in discussions with the United States, cf. ibid., pp. 381-82.

9. Ibid., p. 270.

10. John R. Deane, *Strange Alliance* (New York: Viking, 1947), p. 99.

11. Ibid., p. 98. "It always seemed to me," Deane wrote, "that Mikoyan and his crowd, despite their shrewdness as negotiators, were extremely stupid in not being more cooperative with American representatives in Moscow. I believe that they were incapable of producing facts and figures that would justify any of their requests, because their administrative machinery was not geared to do so. No doubt they conserved considerable manpower by refusing to maintain the statistical records to which we devoted so much time and energy. Nor was careful accounting as essential to them as it was to us. They had only a single front to supply, whereas we had to assess carefully not only the needs of many fronts, but those of many countries. Rather than admit that he could not support his request with facts and figures, Mikoyan took the stand that he need not support them at all. In many cases Averell [Harriman], Sid [Spalding], and I would have been prepared to support the Soviet wishes had they been based on nothing more than a sob story, but even this was not forthcoming—only the haughty statement that 'the Soviet Union requests 50,000 tons of alcohol; therefore she needs it.'"

12. Soviet Master Agreement, Article VII, in *Eighth Quarterly Report to Congress on Lend-Lease Operations,* 78th Congress, 1st Session, House Document No. 129. An identical passage was found

in the British Master Agreement, but it was accepted by the British cabinet only on the understanding that the United Kingdom was not being asked to give up the system of imperial preference in order to obtain Lend-Lease aid. Roosevelt confirmed this understanding in a message to Churchill. (Sherwood, p. 507.)

13. Ibid., p. 574.

14. By November 1941 Russian gross industrial production was less than half what it had been in June 1941. N. A. Voznesensky, *The Economy of the USSR During World War II* (Washington: Public Affairs Press, 1948), p. 24.

15. Harry S. Truman, *Memoirs* (Garden City, N.Y.: Doubleday, 1955), p. 234. Cf. also note 41 to chapter 3, above, on Hull's views.

16. *Twenty-first Report to Congress on Lend-Lease Operations,* for the Period Ended September 30, 1945, p. 25.

17. Ibid.

18. Deane, p. 87.

19. The *Tehran Papers* (see chap. 3, note 30), pp. 490, 500, show that Stalin in the discussion of the military situation referred to his 60-division superiority, but there is no evidence that he said at that time that his troops could be shifted "rapidly" from place to place. On the other hand, Russian superior mobility was clearly a factor in the breakthroughs during the next following year, when German mobility had significantly declined, partly as a result of the western bombing offensive.

20. *Twenty-first Report on Lend Lease Operations,* p. 25.

21. Deane, p. 92.

22. One month before he became President, Harry Truman cast the deciding vote in the extension of the Lend-Lease Act. Truman *Memoirs,* I, 46.

23. Deane, pp. 92-93.

24. Corroboration of this view—that the Russians also expected to obtain shipments remaining from the Lend-Lease program at more favorable prices after the war—is found in the Soviet note of January 3, 1945, where it suggests a "20% discount off the government contracts with firms, of all orders placed before the end of the war and falling under this credit". Cf. above, note 1 to this chapter.

25. *Russian Supply Protocols,* Department of State publication 2759, p. 112.

26. *Yalta Papers*, p. 315.
27. Ibid., p. 318.
28. Ibid., p. 324.
29. Ibid., p. 323.
30. Ibid., pp. 621-22.
31. Ibid., p. 621.
32. Philip E. Mosely, *The Kremlin and World Politics* (New York: Vintage Books, 1960), pp. 176-77.
33. *Hearings Before the Committee on Foreign Relations*, U.S. Senate, 79th Congress, on H. R. 2013, March 28, 1945, pp. 9, 22, and 24.
34. *Yalta Papers*, p. 971.
35. Albert Z. Carr, *Truman, Stalin and Peace* (Garden City, N.Y.: Doubleday, 1950), p. 41. "Although afterward the Russians never ceased to demand that we make good what they called 'Roosevelt's promise' of ten billion of reparations, they certainly sensed at Yalta that there was not much hope for their plan to help revive the Soviet economy at the expense of Germany."

Carr considers that "the question of German reparations may well have been construed by Moscow as a final test of fundamental attitudes in Washington and London. . . . It seems altogether probable that these two matters, an American credit and German reparations, were closely linked in Soviet political thinking, for our attitude toward both questions profoundly affected the rate of Russia's postwar recovery." (Ibid.)

36. The *New York Times* reported that "no answer can be given by the United States to Russia at the present time for two reasons: The Export-Import Bank is limited to loans totalling $700 million, a considerable part of which is already obligated, and again under the terms of the legislation establishing the Bank it is not permissible to lend money to any government which was in default of former payment in April of 1934. There are differences within the Federal Government itself as to whether Russia was in default at that time, some officials arguing that the Soviet Government was obligated to assume the debts acquired in this country by the Kerensky Government and others maintaining that, under law, it wasn't." (January 26, 1945.)

37. *The Forrestal Diaries* (New York: Viking, 1951), p. 41.

38. Ambassador Walter Bedell Smith, in his book, *My Three Years in Moscow* (Philadelphia: Lippincott, 1950), p. 222, recalled that when Secretary of State Marshall saw Stalin on April 15, 1947 and complained about Russian slowness in replying to American communications, Stalin referred to the fate of the January 1945 request for a loan as follows:

" 'With regard to Soviet delays in replying to your representations on various subjects', he [Stalin] continued, 'I would remind Mr. Marshall that more than two years ago the Soviet Government made a request of the United States for a financial credit, and that to date no reply or acknowledgment has ever been received.'

"At this point, I thought it proper to pass to Mr. Molotov a note to remind him that when I came to Moscow I had brought the reply to this request. Mr. Molotov whispered this to Stalin, and received in return a distinct 'family' look. The Generalissimo then corrected his statement accordingly, but remarked that even a year's delay in replying seemed to him to be somewhat excessive."

According to the *New York Times* of March 2, 1946, a Russian request for a $1 billion credit was misplaced "because of errors in transferring the records of the FEA [Foreign Economic Administration] to the custody of the State Department last September" and "turned up only last week." The same paper, on March 3, recalled that "at one point President Truman denied at a press conference, in reply to a question, that the Russians had applied for any credits."

39. *Hearings* on H. R. 2013, March 28, 1945, p. 22.

40. Truman *Memoirs*, p. 228.

41. Ibid., pp. 228-29.

42. Department of State, *Treaties and Other International Acts, Series 3662*, Agreement Between the United States of America and the Union of Soviet Socialist Republics, October 15, 1945, Schedule II, paragraph E.

43. Royal Institute of International Affairs, *America, Britain and Russia—Their Cooperation and Conflict, 1941-1946*, by William Hardy McNeill (London: Oxford University Press, 1953), p. 515.

7

Questions and Answers

QUESTION 1: When the United States and Great Britain defined their war aims in the Atlantic Charter, was the United States at war? ANSWER: No. The Atlantic Charter was signed on August 14, 1941. The United States entered the war on December 7, 1941.

QUESTION 2: Was Russia, which was at war at the time, consulted about this definition of aims? ANSWER: No, Russia was not consulted when the Atlantic Charter was drafted, but it was subsequently asked to adhere.

QUESTION 3: What was the British understanding of the applicability of the Atlantic Charter? ANSWER: Churchill specifically declared that it did not apply to the British Empire. (See note on page x.)

QUESTION 4: When the Soviet Union subscribed to the Atlantic Charter, did it do so without reservation? ANSWER: No. The Soviets entered a reservation that "the practical application of these principles" should be adapted to the "circumstances, needs, and historic peculiarities of particular countries." (See page x.)

QUESTION 5: Did this qualified acceptance of the Atlantic Charter mean that they foreswore the idea of spheres of influence in Europe? ANSWER: No. From the beginning the Russians attempted to get acknowledgment of a privileged position in eastern Europe, for which they were willing in return to acknowledge a privileged British position in western Europe.

QUESTION 6: Was Britain prepared to accept the initial Soviet war aims to the effect that Russia should regain all the territories it had gained as a result of the Nazi-Soviet Pact of 1939? ANSWER: Yes. Churchill considered that this "was the basis on which Russia acceded to the [Atlantic] Charter." (See Chapter 3, note 11.)

QUESTION 7: Why did Britain not give these assurances to the Soviet Union? ANSWER: Because of U. S. objections to any territorial settlement prior to the peace conference. Also, in the U. S. view, such a settlement would not have been in accordance with point two of the Atlantic Charter.

QUESTION 8: After Russia was attacked by Germany in 1941, was the Polish government-in-exile prepared to enter into friendly relations with the Soviet Union? ANSWER: Yes, but only on condition that Russia renounce her war aims and reestablish the Polish state in its pre-1939 boundaries. (See page 41.)

QUESTION 9: Did Russia show any willingness to consider these terms for cooperation with the Polish government-in-exile? ANSWER: No, not even at a time when the Russians were most sorely beset by the invading German armies.

QUESTION 10: What brought about the break between the Soviet Union and the Polish government-in-exile? ANSWER: The discovery by the Germans of the bodies of murdered Polish officers, which led the Poles in London to call for an investigation by the International Red Cross.

QUESTION 11: What was Churchill's reaction to the Polish call for a Red Cross investigation? ANSWER: He thought it a mistake. He said to the premier of the Polish exile government: "If they are dead nothing you can do will bring them back." (Chapter 3, note 18.)

QUESTION 12: What was the opinion of George Kennan on the action of the Polish government-in-exile which brought the break with the Soviet Union? ANSWER: "It is hard, in retrospect, to see how the Poles could have done less."

QUESTION 13: On the basis of all the evidence that has become available since that time, does it look as if the story about the Katyn massacre was a Nazi provocation? ANSWER: The weight of evidence is that the Polish officers in question were killed by the Russians, but there is reason to believe that this was the result of a mistake. (See page 45.)

QUESTION 14: What, subsequently, was the principal obstacle to reestablishment of relations between the Soviet Union and the Polish government-in-exile? ANSWER: The question of Poland's eastern border. Neither the Soviets nor the Polish exiles were willing to accept, or even discuss, the view of the other side on this question.

QUESTION 15: What was the position of the London Poles with respect to the impending entry into Poland of Russian troops as they were driving the Germans back toward Germany? ANSWER: They threatened to call upon the Polish underground to resist the Russians if they advanced into Poland without a prior agreement with the government-in-exile.

QUESTION 16: What did Russia next propose with respect to the postwar frontiers of Poland? ANSWER: At the Tehran Conference, Stalin proposed that in return for acceptance of the eastern borders of 1939, Poland should be compensated by getting German territory up to the Oder River.

QUESTION 17: What was the American reaction to this proposal? ANSWER: There was no official American reaction to this proposal at the Conference. But Roosevelt privately explained to Stalin that he was worried about the reaction of Americans of Polish extraction.

QUESTION 18: What was the British reaction to this proposal? ANSWER: Churchill agreed with it in general terms, subject to some modifications of Poland's eastern frontier in favor of Poland.

QUESTION 19: How did Churchill attempt to persuade the Polish exile government to accept this new territorial arrangement? ANSWER: He repeatedly urged it upon Mikolajczyk. He said that if the exiles did not act quickly, he "could not be responsible for anything that might take place."

QUESTION 20: By the time the Russians reached the old Polish frontier, would they have been satisfied with an agreement on the territorial question? ANSWER: No, by this time they had started to talk about the need for a "friendly" (i.e., Communist-dominated) Polish government. (See page 53.)

QUESTION 21: By the time the Russian forces were in territory which Russia itself recognized as Polish, what was the Russian position? ANSWER: It had hardened further. Now the Russians asked not only for acceptance of their territorial position, but they set up a puppet organization, the so-called Lublin Committee, which they said must furnish the majority of any Polish government.

QUESTION 22: Why did the U. S. government not take a vigorous and clear-cut position on these issues at that time? ANSWER: Because, as Roosevelt had stated, he was concerned about the Polish-American vote in the 1944 elections; and also, as Hull stated later, because the United States needed Russian military cooperation in view of the forthcoming invasion of western Europe.

QUESTION 23: Who were the leaders of the Polish uprising against the Germans in Warsaw, which the Russians refused to support? ANSWER: They were exponents of the government-in-exile.

QUESTION 24: What is McNeill's opinion about the failure to resolve the Polish question at that time? ANSWER: "The failure of Allied policy to achieve a peaceable settlement of the Polish problem in the first seven months of 1944 may well be considered the turning-point in the history of the Grand Alliance." (Chapter 3, note 42.)

QUESTION 25: Who was in control of Poland at the time of the Yalta Conference? ANSWER: The Red Army had occupied almost all of prewar Poland.

QUESTION 26: What was agreed at Yalta with respect to Poland's frontiers? ANSWER: While the United States did not agree on the western frontiers, the eastern frontier was in effect settled substantially along the lines of the original Russian position.

QUESTION 27: What did the West get out of this belated acceptance of the Soviet position on its western border? ANSWER: Nothing. But some Western participants apparently thought that they had obtained Russian agreement to a democratic rump Poland.

QUESTION 28: How about the famous Declaration on Liberated Europe? Was this not a quid pro quo for acceptance of the Soviet border proposal? ANSWER: It was hardly discussed at Yalta and the operative clause was watered down by the Russians so that it provided only for "mutual consultation" instead of the "machinery for the carrying out of the joint responsibilities" which the United States had proposed. (See Chapter 4, note 18.) However, the United States attached great importance to the principles laid down in that document. (See also Questions 55 and 56.)

QUESTION 29: What was agreed at Yalta with respect to the Polish government? ANSWER: It was agreed that the existing (Communist) government would be "reorganized" into a new, fully representative government and that that government should be "pledged to the holding of free and unfettered elections."

QUESTION 30: What was the Russian interpretation of this agreement? ANSWER: It was that only Poles who had agreed to the Yalta territorial decisions could participate in the reorganized government, and that only a few non-Communist Poles could be included in the provisional government.

QUESTION 31: In the ensuing arguments between the Western Allies and Russia, what was the Western position? ANSWER: That the Yalta Agreement called for a completely new Polish government and that a veto on some prospective participants violated the very foundation of the Yalta Agreement.

QUESTION 32: What was Roosevelt's personal view about the position? ANSWER: He had doubts about it, at least on one occasion. As he wrote Churchill, he was aware that under the Yalta agreement "somewhat more emphasis" would be placed on the Lublin (Communist) Poles. (See page 90.)

QUESTION 33: Did the Polish exile leaders agree with the Western position on this matter? ANSWER: Not entirely. Some of them actually felt, like the Russians, that the Yalta Agreement had in effect conceded that the new Polish government would be dominated by the Communists. (See Chapter 4, note 29.)

QUESTION 34: What was President Truman's position on this matter? ANSWER: It was that the Russians were violating the

Questions and Answers

Yalta Agreement and that the agreement could not be interpreted as involving the establishment of a Communist-dominated provisional Polish government.

QUESTION 35: What was the Russian reaction to this position? ANSWER: It was that it amounted to "abrogation" of the Yalta decisions.

QUESTION 36: How did the Hopkins mission contribute to a solution of this issue? ANSWER: It opened the way for the eventual establishment of a Communist-dominated provisional Polish government. (See Chapter 4, note 41.)

QUESTION 37: Did the Russians live up to their obligation to cause "free and unfettered elections" to be held in Poland? ANSWER: No. Elections were held only in 1947, after the non-Communist parties had been thoroughly terrorized.

QUESTION 38: What was the American position on spheres of influence in Europe? ANSWER: The United States was strongly opposed to them. Secretary of State Hull stated that he felt that Russia's security could be better guaranteed by a "strong postwar peace organization." (See Chapter 5, note 3.)

QUESTION 39: What was the first country liberated or occupied by the Allies (then called United Nations) in the war? ANSWER: Italy, whose surrender was accepted "by authority of the Governments of the United States and Great Britain and in the interest of the United Nations."

QUESTION 40: What was the Russian position on their role in the political direction of the occupation of Italy? ANSWER: They wanted a full role in it.

QUESTION 41: What was the U. S.-British response to this? ANSWER: The request was very poorly received, and the Russians were excluded from the Control Commission. When an "Inter-Allied Advisory Council" was later established, it had no role in determining occupation policies.

QUESTION 42: Did this not imply that the Western Allies in

fact viewed the territories conquered or liberated by them as an exclusive sphere of influence? ANSWER: Yes, at least as far as the wartime period was concerned, but there is no evidence that this was ever explicitly stated as policy.

QUESTION 43: What was the reason for this Western position? ANSWER: The United States and Britain did not wish the Russians to have a role in the occupation of Italy because they were worried that the Russians would support the activities of the Italian Communists; and there is good evidence that that worry was justified.

QUESTION 44: When the United States and Britain later demanded a share in determining occupation policies in Rumania, what was the Russian reaction? ANSWER: The Russians refused, referring to Italy as a precedent.

QUESTION 45: What was the real Russian reason? ANSWER: There is no evidence for this, but quite probably they were afraid that the United States and Britain would support the activities of the anti-Communists.

QUESTION 46: What, then, was the difference between the situation in Italy and in Rumania? ANSWER: In Italy, the Western Allies were pretty sure that in free elections the anti-Communists, whom they favored, would win. In Rumania, the Russians had good reason to fear that in free elections the Communists, whom they favored, would lose.

QUESTION 47: How did the Russians in fact use their predominance in occupied Rumania? ANSWER: They forced a Communist-dominated government on King Michael.

QUESTION 48: When Churchill was prepared, early in 1944, to recognize Russian ("temporary") predominance in Rumania in return for their recognition of similar British predominance in Greece, what was the American reaction? ANSWER: The United States spiked the deal on the ground that it would conflict with the basic declarations of postwar aims and would create a dangerous precedent.

QUESTION 49: When Churchill finally in October 1944 made an agreement with Stalin that in effect established spheres of influence in the Balkans, what was the American reaction? ANSWER: The United States acquiesced in the deal but four months later, at Yalta, it was nullified by the Declaration on Liberated Europe which substituted broad general principles for the pragmatic and temporary arrangement between Churchill and Stalin.

QUESTION 50: What was the immediate effect of the spheres-of-influence arrangement on the British position in Greece? ANSWER: It was most favorable, and Churchill subsequently (at Yalta) expressed his thanks to Stalin for "not having taken too great an interest in Greek affairs."

QUESTION 51: What was the effect of the Churchill-Stalin agreement on the situation in Yugoslavia? ANSWER: Britain and Russia jointly tried to create a coalition government. Stalin encouraged Churchill to move British troops into northwestern Yugoslavia.

QUESTION 52: What was Tito's position with regard to a British military operation in Yugoslavia? ANSWER: He was violently opposed to it. This did not, however, prevent the Russians from reiterating their proposal three months later, at the Yalta Conference.

QUESTION 53: Did the Churchill-Stalin agreement in fact result in a 50:50 division of influence in Yugoslavia? ANSWER: It did not, and Churchill complained about this, albeit rather weakly.

QUESTION 54: What credence should be given to Stalin's statement at Yalta that he had little influence on Tito? ANSWER: From evidence that has become available after Yugoslavia defected from the Soviet bloc, it appears that Tito in any case strongly resented the Churchill-Stalin agreement.

QUESTION 55: Was the Declaration on Liberated Europe which was signed at Yalta put into effect by the Russians? ANSWER: No. The principles of joint assistance to the people of the European liberated states or former Axis satellites, especially as regards the formation of "broadly representative governments" and the facilitating of free elections, were largely ignored.

QUESTION 56: In the opinion of the signatories, did the Declaration on Liberated Europe extinguish the spheres-of-influence deal which Churchill and Stalin had concluded in October 1944? ANSWER: As far as the United States is concerned, the answer is clearly in the affirmative; but we cannot be sure that the Russians felt the same way. The anomalous situation in Hungary after Yalta suggests that the spirit of the October 1944 deal may have lingered on for quite some time.

QUESTION 57: In what respects was the situation in Hungary (where Churchill and Stalin had agreed on a 50:50 division of influence) "anomalous"? ANSWER: Hungary is the only Russian-occupied country where relatively free elections, resulting in a non-Communist majority, were permitted in 1945. (The Soviet-occupied zone of Austria was another such situation.)

QUESTION 58: But was not Hungary taken over by the Communists with Russian military support? ANSWER: Yes, but this took place only in 1947, long after the Cold War had begun. In 1945, the Russians had apparently not yet made up their mind on this matter. Perhaps they might then have been amenable to some bargaining, but this was never explored.

QUESTION 59: What did the United States have available for such bargaining? How about the threat of force? ANSWER: Roosevelt at Yalta said he did not believe American troops would stay in Europe much more than two years after the war.

QUESTION 60: What other bargaining counter might the United States have used in order to exercise a mitigating role at least in such countries as Hungary, Czechoslovakia, and Austria, where Russian predominance had not been accepted by Churchill? ANSWER: Credits, in which the Russians were very interested in view of the devastation they had suffered in the war.

QUESTION 61: Did the Russians have reason to expect that American goods would be available to them on favorable terms after the war? ANSWER: Yes. There was much talk about the expected great American postwar "surplus." The chairman of the U. S. War Production Board and the president of the U. S. Chamber of Commerce ventilated the idea of large postwar credits in their talks with Russian leaders.

QUESTION 62: What was the approximate value of the U. S. "Lend-Lease" aid to Russia during the war? ANSWER: Nine and one-half billion dollars.

QUESTION 63: How was this aid used as leverage during the delicate negotiations with the Russians at the end of the war? ANSWER: It was not used at all. The aid was suddenly cut off in a manner which President Truman (who later rescinded the order) described as one that "made it appear as if somebody had been deliberately snubbed."

QUESTION 64: During the period immediately prior to the Yalta Conference, did Russia apply for a loan for postwar reconstruction? ANSWER: Yes, on January 3, 1945, Russia formally asked for a six billion dollar loan at $2\frac{1}{4}$ per cent interest.

QUESTION 65: Is there evidence that Roosevelt intended to use economic aid as a diplomatic instrument in his negotiations with Stalin? ANSWER: Yes, but it is not conclusive. Apparently he intended to discuss the matter at Yalta. Also, there is a memorandum in which Roosevelt noted that the Russians "in their occupied territories will do more or less what they wish" and went on to say that he did not intend to "break off or delay negotiations" over future Lend-Lease deliveries. (Chapter 6, notes 5 and 29.)

QUESTION 66: Was either the future of Lend-Lease or the Russian request for a six-billion-dollar credit actually used for bargaining purposes at the Yalta Conference? ANSWER: No. Neither of these two matters came up between Roosevelt and Stalin during any of their discussions at Yalta, where the greatest amount of time had to be devoted to Poland.

QUESTION 67: In what other way did the Russians attempt to lay their hands on substantial amounts of capital to help in their reconstruction? ANSWER: Through German reparations, which they wished to fix at $20 billion at Yalta, with half of that amount to go to the Soviet Union.

QUESTION 68: At that time, did the United States have a reparations policy? ANSWER: No. Roosevelt left the lead to Churchill, who opposed such large reparations; but in the end Roosevelt agreed to use the $20 billion figure "as a basis for discussion."

QUESTION 69: Was there contemporary diplomatic opinion that there must have been a link in the Russian mind between their request for exorbitant German reparations and their hope for an American credit? ANSWER: Ambassador Winant "urged at the time that the U. S. consider ways of helping the recovery of the Soviet economy, such assistance to be linked to the achievement of a satisfactory settlement of the problem of German reparations and of the most important political issues between the two Governments." (See page 164.)

QUESTION 70: What other opinion is there available on this

probable link? ANSWER: Carr has stated: "It seems altogether probable that these two matters, an American credit and German reparations, were closely linked in Soviet political thinking, for our attitude toward both questions profoundly affected the rate of Russia's postwar recovery." (Chapter 6, note 35.)

QUESTION 71: Could the Russian loan request have been handled under the heading of Lend-Lease? ANSWER: No, there was strong Congressional sentiment against the use of Lend-Lease for postwar assistance, and a limitation to that effect was actually written into the law in April, 1945. A majority in favor of renewal of the Lend-Lease Act was obtained in the Senate earlier in 1945 only when Vice President Truman broke a tie vote.

QUESTION 72: Why did negotiations for a "Supplementary Agreement" governing credit sales of Lend-Lease equipment to be used for postwar reconstruction fail to bring agreement in the early months of 1945? ANSWER: The Russians insisted on an interest rate of 2 per cent, whereas the U. S. negotiators would not budge from their position that it must be no less than $2\frac{3}{8}$ per cent.

QUESTION 73: What really lay behind that difference in interest rates? ANSWER: Differing views on tactics. The Russians apparently thought that the fear of postwar unemployment would cause the United States to yield. The American negotiators were apparently oblivious of the leverage that might be sought in noneconomic matters, and they only feared that the United States would seem overly eager for postwar trade if it acceded to the Russian terms. (Chapter 6, notes 26 and 27.)

QUESTION 74: What finally caused the Russian loan request to be lost in the Washington bureaucracy? ANSWER: The opinion of legal experts that a loan to Russia would contravene a law which ruled out loans to countries that had defaulted on earlier loans—and the Soviet Union had long ago repudiated the debts of the Kerensky government. (Chapter 6, note 26.)

QUESTION 75: What was the real reason for the failure of interest to develop in the U. S. government for some settlement that might include the loan sought by the Soviets? ANSWER: The growing disillusionment with Russia over the issue of Poland and the other east European occupied territories. Poland was the major issue between Russia and the West when Truman became President.

QUESTION 76: In the absence of any other means of satisfying the urgent Soviet need for capital assets to further their reconstruction, what was the consequence of Allied disagreements over German reparations? ANSWER: The partition of Germany, brought about—among other reasons—by the Soviet desire to plunder that country.

QUESTION 77: But was not the partition of Germany a cause of the Cold War? ANSWER: Under this analysis, it was not a cause but a consequence. By the time of Potsdam (July 1945), it was clear that the Western powers would not accept the de facto Russian sphere of influence in eastern Europe and that they had nothing to offer Russia to make it forgo the establishment of such a sphere also in central Europe.

QUESTION 78: When was the die then cast and the Cold War begun? ANSWER: In the period between Yalta and Potsdam, when the division of Europe was in effect determined by the relationship of military power as it existed at the time, and when the United States failed to throw into the balance its economic power, which was later to play such an important role in the conduct of the Cold War.

8

Comments in Retrospect

McGEORGE BUNDY:

It is now fashionable in this country to look back at Yalta as
a time of wishful thinking, in which American statesmen were
outsmarted by Stalin. Critics of Yalta have never shown that
Mr. Roosevelt or Mr. Churchill granted anything that they were
in a position to withhold (except perhaps the Kurile Islands).
The object of the western statesmen at Yalta was to persuade
Stalin that the common interest required genuine cooperation
on the basis of self-restraint by the Great Powers. It seemed for
a moment that he was persuaded. In the event, we have seen
that he was not. Perhaps the western statesmen, and the peoples
whom, in this, they truly represented, should not have believed
peaceful cooperation between Russia and the rest of the world
a practical possibilty, but it is hard to deny their central conviction: that such cooperation would have been to the great
advantage of all concerned. In any event, they did in fact ob-

tain agreements which, if kept, would have amounted to a pledge of lasting peace. . . .

The men in the Kremlin had three choices after Yalta. One was to accept its principles and to devote themselves to the construction of a sincere peace, based on mutual respect for vital interests, and self-restraint in other areas. The second was to pretend to accept the Yalta principles—in other words, to make an effort to conserve the advantages of the reservoir of good will—while continuing under the surface the great contest for the world ordained by Stalinist theory. It may be that Soviet leaders thought this was in fact the course they were following. But the course that seems most nearly to fit the actual record of Soviet behavior since Yalta is a third one—a policy characterized by an apparent decision to disregard as unimportant the good will of the non-Communist west and to proceed as energetically as possible to expand and consolidate Communist power.

Quoted, by permission, from "The Test of Yalta," *Foreign Affairs,* Vol. 27, No. 4 (July, 1949).

GENERAL PATRICK J. HURLEY:

America was in a position at Yalta to speak the only language the Communists understand, the language of power. The President of the United States at Yalta was in command of the greatest land, navy and air force ever assembled on earth. One quiet sentence to Marshal Stalin in that language could have indicated that America would require him to keep his solemn agreements. That one sentence would have prevented the conquest of all the Balkan states, the conquest of Poland, and the conquest of China. The sentence was not forthcoming. On the contrary, your diplomats and mine surrendered in secret every principle for which we said we were fighting. They talk about Stalin breaking his agreements, gentlemen. He never had to break one. We cowardly surrendered to him everything that he had signed and we did it in secret. President Roosevelt was already a sick man at Yalta.

Hearings before the Committee on Armed Services and the Committee on Foreign Relations, U.S. Senate, *To Conduct an Inquiry Into the Military Situation in the Far East and the Facts Surrounding the Relief of General of the Army Douglas MacArthur from His Assignment in that Area* (June, 1951), p. 2839.

PROFESSOR HANS J. MORGENTHAU:

The Yalta agreements in particular were an attempt, doomed to failure from the outset, to maintain a modicum of Western influence in the nations of Eastern Europe which the Red Army had conquered. That influence was to be maintained through the instrument of free, democratic elections. Yet in view of the fear and hatred with which most of Eastern Europe has traditionally reacted to the colossus from the East, free elections in Eastern Europe could be considered by the Soviet Union only as a weapon with which first to limit, and then to destroy, Soviet control. Thus it was utopian to expect that the Soviet Union would jeopardize its conquests in order to make good on a legal promise to a competitor who had lost his ability to enforce such a promise on the battlefields of the Second World War.

Quoted, by permission, from "The End of an Illusion," *Commentary,* November, 1961.

AMBASSADOR W. AVERELL HARRIMAN:

The most difficult question to answer is why Stalin took so many commitments which he subsequently failed to honor.

191

There can be no clear answer to this question. I believe that the Kremlin had two approaches to their post-war policies and in my many talks with Stalin I felt that he himself was of two minds. One approach emphasized reconstruction and development of Russia and the other external expansion.

On the one hand they were discussing a possible understanding with us which would lead to peaceful relations and result in increased trade and loans from the West for the reconstruction of the terrible devastation left in the wake of the war. If they had carried out this program they would have had to soft-pedal, for the time at least, the communist designs for world domination—much along the lines of the policies they had pursued between the two wars.

On the other hand, we had constant difficulties with them throughout the war and they treated us with great suspicion. Moreover, there were indications that they would take advantage of the Red Army occupation of neighboring countries to maintain control, and they were supporting Communist parties in other countries to be in a position to take control in the post-war turmoil.

The Kremlin chose the second course. It is my belief that Stalin was influenced by the hostile attitude of the peoples of Eastern Europe toward the Red Army and that he recognized that governments established by free elections would not be "friendly" to the Soviet Union. In addition, I believe he became increasingly aware of the great opportunities for Soviet expansion in the post-war economic chaos. After our rapid demobilization I do not think that he conceived that the United States would take the firm stand that we have taken in the past five years.

Hearings before the Committee on Armed Services and the Committee on Foreign Relations, U. S. Senate, *To Conduct an Inquiry Into the Military Situation in the Far East and the Facts Surrounding*

Comments in Retrospect

the Relief of General of the Army Douglas MacArthur from His Assignment in that Area (July, 1951), pp. 3341-3342.

EDWARD R. STETTINIUS, JR., former Secretary of State:

From my close association with Franklin D. Roosevelt, I know that he was primarily motivated by the great ideal of friendly cooperation among nations. At the same time he had no illusions about the dangers and difficulties of dealing with the Soviet Union. He emphasized many times that we must keep trying with patience and determination to get the Russians to realize that it was in their own selfish interest to win the confidence of the other countries of the world. . . . It was essential that Prime Minister Churchill and President Roosevelt made an honest attempt at Yalta to work with the Russians. For the peace of the world, they had to make every effort to test the good faith of the Soviet Union. Until agreements were made and tested, the world could not clearly know of the difficulties of securing Russian compliance with agreements.

Quoted, by permission, from *Roosevelt and the Russians—The Yalta Conference* (New York: Doubleday, 1949), pp. 322 and 324.

PROFESSOR PHILIP E. MOSELY:

In hindsight, it is easy to say that the attempt [to cooperate with the Soviet Union] was hopeless and not worth making because the Soviet leadership would never abate its claims to reshape the world in its own image or forego any immediate and material advantage for the sake of retaining the good will of what it regarded as temporary allies. Still, it is to the credit of Western statesmen that they made many efforts to offer postwar cooperation among equals in the hope that Stalin would grant this breathing spell to the sorely tried people of the Soviet Union. To make the cooperation stick, much more should have been done to assure him of assistance in rebuilding the Soviet economy; as it turned out, Stalin and the Soviet people soon felt that their vast sacrifices were forgotten by less war-damaged allies as soon as the fighting was over. That and other policies would have required a much more integrated strategy than American policy-makers seemed capable of achieving during World War II.

Quoted, by permission, from *The Kremlin in World Politics* (New York: Vintage Books, 1960), pp. 155-56.

SENATOR ROBERT A. TAFT:

Power without foresight leads to disaster. Our international relations have been conducted with so little foresight since 1941 that six years after vast military victories in Europe and Asia we face a more dangerous threat than any that has menaced us before. Our soldiers, sailors, marines, and airmen have not failed us. Our political leaders have. By 1941 anyone who was not bamboozled by Soviet psychological warfare knew that the Soviet Government was a predatory totalitarian tyranny intent on establishing Communist dictatorship throughout the world. But our leaders failed to foresee that the Soviet Union would turn against us after the defeat of Germany and Japan. They made no attempt to insure our future against that eventuality. They brought forth no positive policy for the creation of a free and united Europe or for the preservation of the independence of China. They preferred wishful thinking to facts, and convinced themselves that Stalin would co-operate with them to create a free world of permanent peace. So at Teheran, Yalta,

194

and Potsdam they handed Stalin the freedom of Eastern Europe and Manchuria, and prepared our present peril.

Quoted, by permission, from *A Foreign Policy for Americans* (Garden City, N.Y.: Doubleday, 1951), p. 6.

WALTER LIPPMANN:

The terms of the problem were defined at Yalta in the winter of 1945. There, with a victory over Germany in sight, Roosevelt, Churchill, and Stalin made a military settlement which fixed the boundaries where the converging armies were to meet, and were to wait while the governments negotiated the terms of peace which would provide for the withdrawal of the armies. The crucial issue in the world today [1947] is whether the Yalta military boundary, which was intended to be provisional for the period of the armistice, is to become the political boundary of two hostile coalitions.

The Yalta line registered an agreed estimate by Roosevelt, Churchill, and Stalin as to what would be the actual military situation at the close of hostilities. They knew that the Red Army would be in Warsaw, Bucharest, Budapest, Belgrade and Sofia. So Churchill and Roosevelt recognized that the military boundary for the armistice would place eastern Europe within the Soviet sphere. The British, on the other hand, were in Athens; the British-Americans were in Italy; therefore, Stalin recognized that Italy and Greece would be within the British and American sphere. . . .

The British and Americans, of course, could not accept the permanent division of the European continent along the Yalta line. They could not accept a settlement in which Poland, Czechoslovakia, Yugoslavia, Hungary, Rumania and Bulgaria would lose all independence and become incorporated as Soviet republics in the U. S. S. R. They had a debt of honor to the countless patriots in those lands. They realized that if the frontiers of the Soviet system were extended as far west as the middle of Germany and Austria, then not only Germany and Austria but all western Europe might fall within the Russian sphere of influence and be dominated by the Soviet Union.

Thus for the best of reasons and with the best of motives they came to the conclusion that they must wage a diplomatic campaign to prevent Russia from expanding her sphere, to prevent her from consolidating it, and to compel her to contract it. But they failed to see clearly that until the Red Army evacuated eastern Europe and withdrew to the frontiers of the Soviet Union, none of these objectives could be achieved.

Had they seen clearly the significance of the military situation, they would not have committed the United States to anything in eastern Europe while the Soviet government had the power to oppose it, while the United States had no power to enforce it. They would have taken and noted the pledges and promises to respect the independence and the freedom of the nations of eastern Europe which Stalin gave them at Yalta. But they would not have committed the United States to a guarantee that Stalin would keep his pledges while his army was occupying eastern Europe.

For since the United States could not make good this guarantee, the onus of the violation of the pledges was divided between the Russians, who broke them, and the Americans, who had promised to enforce them and did not. It would have been far better to base our policy on the realities of the balance of power, to let Stalin, who made the promises which he alone could fulfill, take the whole responsibility for breaking them; to concentrate our effort on treaties of peace which would end the occupation of Europe.

Comments in Retrospect

Quoted, by permission, from *The Cold War—A Study in U.S. Foreign Policy* (New York: Harper, 1947), pp. 35-37.

ISAAC DON LEVINE:

The road to Teheran, Yalta and Berlin has from its very inception witnessed a race between President Roosevelt's pursuit of Soviet cooperation within the framework of a world organization and Stalin's unrelenting efforts to expand, through seizure and aggrandizement, the Soviet realm. While Roosevelt was busy building the peace of tomorrow, Stalin was preying upon his smaller and weaker neighbors in both Europe and Asia, from Finland to Iran.

This race is the pivot of the history of our days. It is a race between direct action and devious policy. For President Roosevelt never directly challenged the unilateral performance of Moscow. Instead he pressed more and more for the creation of international machinery to checkmate such action. However, the more Roosevelt sought to pin Stalin down through the device of a world organization, the more hurried and frequent became Stalin's overt and covert acts of expansion. Through such procedure Stalin had carved out for himself a vast new domain in Europe while the atmosphere of the great democracies reverberated with the song of international cooperation. By the time the Yalta conference convened, even the blind could see that Soviet unilateral action was making a mockery of world cooperation. President Roosevelt had to go to Yalta. He went determined to win the race against Stalin—by bringing into being his world organization for peace. . . .

In this setting and against this background it was inevitable that out of Yalta would come a high-sounding document serving as a cover for surrender to Stalin on all substantial issues.

Beginnings of the Cold War

Quoted, by permission, from "Yalta Aftermath," *American Affairs*, Vol. 7, No. 3 (July, 1945), National Industrial Conference Board, Inc., New York.

PROFESSOR WILLIAM HARDY MCNEILL:

Whatever doubts there must be about Stalin's attitude to European revolution, there were none about his territorial aims. Throughout the war he had asserted that the territories he had annexed in 1939 and 1940 from Poland, Rumania, and Finland were permanently and legally his; and that the countries of Lithuania, Latvia, and Estonia, annexed in 1940, had become member republics of the Soviet Union. Improvement of the military security of Russia's western frontier was no doubt an important consideration which persuaded Stalin to take this position. Prestige was another factor. Stalin was no more than reasserting Russian authority over territories which had long recognized Tsarist rule, and which had been torn away from Russia at the time of her revolutionary weakness after the First World War. Finally, as far as the eastern provinces of pre-war Poland were concerned, Stalin may well have felt the need to pacify Ukranian and White Russian national feeling. At least he said so; and, in view of the rather delicate relationship which had existed between the Ukraine and Great Russia since the days of the Bolshevik Revolution, Stalin may have been speaking honestly.

Unfortunately for Stalin's political programme, there was a potential contradiction between his purposes in Eastern Europe and his hope of remaining on good terms with America and Britain. . . .

What Stalin conceived to be the future role of the Communist parties in the countries neighboring Russia cannot be stated

198

with any certainty. The Soviet Government disclaimed on several occasions any intention of revolutionizing the social order, in Poland or in other adjacent countries. Stalin told Mikolajczyk in October 1944: "Communism does not fit the Poles. They are too individualistic, too nationalistic. . . . Poland will be a capitalist state." . . . It is impossible to be sure that Stalin was frank in making statements such as these; but his day-to-day policy suggests that throughout 1944 he hoped to come to satisfactory terms with non-Communist groups in Poland, Rumania, and other countries similarly situated. . . . Perhaps Stalin hoped that Communist Parties would be sufficiently strong after the war to check by a sort of internal veto any anti-Russian tendencies that might arise in the governments of Europe, and wished no more than that for the immediate future.

If this is a fair statement of Stalin's aims—and in the nature of the case it is highly speculative—he no doubt hoped that they would prove acceptable to the Western Powers. Indeed, Britain and America might well have agreed to Stalin's programme if he had been able to persuade the Poles, Rumanians, and others to accept the role he had assigned to them; but as it turned out he was not able to do so without resort to high-handed intervention and brutal disregard of the niceties of democratic government.

As between the friendship of the Western Powers and a secure politico-military position on his western frontier, Stalin chose the latter. He probably never made the choice in any deliberate and cold-blooded manner. Rather, insisting upon the security of his frontiers, he little by little sacrificed the sympathy of Britain and America. . . .

Quoted, by permission, from *America, Britain and Russia—Their Co-Operation and Conflict, 1941-1946*, Royal Institute of International Affairs (London: Oxford University Press, 1953), pp. 406-408.

Beginnings of the Cold War

Ambassador George F. Kennan:

Once we had come into the European war, and granted the heavy military handicaps with which the Western powers were then confronted in that theater, the decisions taken throughout the remainder of the war years were those of harried, over-worked men, operating in the vortex of a series of tremendous pressures, military and otherwise, which we today find it difficult to remember or to imagine. I think that some injustice is being done both to the men in question and to the cause of historical understanding by the latter-day interpretations which regard specific decisions of the wartime years as the source of all our present difficulties. The most vociferous charges of war-time mistakes relate primarily to our dealings with the U. S. S. R. and particularly to the wartime conferences of Moscow, Teheran, and Yalta.

As one who was very unhappy about these conferences at the time they were taking place and very worried lest they lead to false hopes and misunderstandings, I may perhaps be permitted to say that I think their importance has recently been considerably overrated. If it cannot be said that the Western democracies gained very much from these talks with the Russians, it would also be incorrect to say that they gave very much away. The establishment of Soviet military power in eastern Europe and the entry of Soviet forces into Manchuria was not the result of these talks; it was the result of the military operations during the concluding phases of the war. There was nothing the Western democracies could have done to prevent the Russians from entering these areas except to get there first, and this we were not in a position to do. . . .

. . . in all these matters we must bear in mind both the overriding compulsion of military necessity under which our states-men were working and also the depth of their conviction that one had no choice but to gamble on the possibility that Soviet suspicions might be broken down and Soviet collaboration won for the postwar period, if there were to be any hope of perma-nent peace. Many of us who were familiar with Russian matters were impatient with this line of thought at the time, because we knew how poor were the chances of success, and we saw no reason why a Western world which kept its nerves, its good humor, and a due measure of military preparedness should not continue indefinitely to live in the same world with the power of the Kremlin without flying to either of the extremes of polit-ical intimacy or war.

In the light of what has occurred subsequently, I can see that our view, too, was not fully rounded. We were right about the nature of Soviet power; but we were wrong about the ability of American democracy at this stage in its history to bear for long a situation full of instability, inconvenience, and military danger. Perhaps Harry Hopkins and F. D. R. had more reason than we then supposed to believe that everything depended on the possibility of changing the attitude of the Soviet regime. But, if so, this is then only an indication that the dilemma was crueler than any of us really appreciated. . . .

Quoted, by permission, from *American Diplomacy—1900-1950* (Chicago: University of Chicago Press, 1951), pp. 84-87.

PROFESSOR NORMAN A. GRAEBNER:

Only the most astute observers during the war could see that the United States, in its pursuit of total victory, was helping to create a new balance of power that would prove to be as unac-ceptable as that created by Hitler. Any return to normalcy required a Russian withdrawal to its prewar boundaries and, in general, its prewar status in world affairs—to be achieved quite automatically through the Soviet acceptance of the principle of self-determination of peoples. Fundamentally, the Atlantic Charter promised a postwar world without permanent victors or permanent losers. For the American people, having suffered no invasion, this was both a feasible and a moral arrangement. . . .

Unfortunately, the well-established facts of international life scarcely warranted the Western expectation of a new world order based on the Wilsonian principles of justice and self-determination. Throughout the war it was clear that Allied interests coincided only on the issue of defeating the common enemy. The United States and Great Britain entered the war as satiated powers, seeking nothing but peace and stability in world affairs. They had written their moral and limited purpose into the Atlantic Charter as early as August, 1941. For the Kremlin this repudiation of the tangible and lasting emoluments of victory was never an acceptable basis of action. Whether Russia eventually signed the Atlantic Charter or not, she would not settle for a world based on the principle of self-determination. Any assumption that she would expected too much denial of that country's historic problems and ambitions.

Quoted, by permission, from *Cold War Diplomacy, 1945-1960* (Princeton, N.J.: Van Nostrand, 1962), pp. 8 and 13.

PROFESSOR JOHN L. SNELL:

The genuine hope of Roosevelt and Churchill for postwar cooperation with the U. S. S. R. proved to be an illusion, but even this hope was virtually imposed by necessity. Knowing that the only alternative to cooperation in the postwar world would be an outright war or lasting and costly vigilance against the U. S. S. R., both of the Western leaders were prepared to make some concessions to obtain Stalin's enduring cooperation. "The only hope for the world," Churchill wrote as late as January, 1945, "is the agreement of the three Great Powers. If they quarrel, our children are undone." . . . If Roosevelt had refused to work for this return to "normalcy" he would have won certain condemnation by the American people. But he could not try for a return to peaceful conditions and at the same time plan for a crusade against Communist Russia.

How deeply Roosevelt really *believed* in the possibility of postwar cooperation with the U. S. S. R. is impossible to know; his saying that he had a "hunch" that Stalin would cooperate is scarcely proof of strong conviction, nor are wartime avowals of his faith in Stalin; Churchill himself once commented that he "felt bound to proclaim his confidence in Soviet good faith in the hope of securing it." Certainly Roosevelt hoped that cooperation would be possible but, hope or no hope, he *had* to work for it, given the expectations of the American people. They would be made willing to assume continuing global responsibilities in peacetime only by the clear demonstration between 1944 and 1947 that Stalin's expansion could be curbed in no other way. It can be left to those who enjoy the Cold War—if there be any—to say that the wartime efforts to cooperate with Stalin should never have been made or should not have been carried as far as they were.

Quoted, by permission, from *Illusion and Necessity: The Diplomacy of Global War 1939-1945* (Boston: Houghton Mifflin, 1963), pp. 212-13.

Principal Sources

(Numbers refer to the notes to the respective chapters, where the full title of each work, its publisher, and date of publication are first stated.)

Wherever possible, I have relied on primary sources, but a number of signposts to the documentary material have been invaluable.

There are two especially useful surveys of the wartime dealings between Russia and the West: William H. McNeill's *America, Britain and Russia—Their Cooperation and Conflict, 1941-1946* (ch.3, n.7) and Herbert Feis's *Churchill, Roosevelt, Stalin—The War They Waged and the Peace They Sought* (ch.1, n.6). Of these, McNeill's book is the more useful for research purposes because it contains more factual information and is painstakingly provided with references to the primary sources. On the other hand, Feis has written much the more readable book. Although I have not had recourse to it, mention should also be made of John L. Snell's compact *Illusion and Necessity—The Diplomacy of Global War, 1939-1945,* which was published subsequently, but from which a perceptive passage is quoted in Chapter 8. -

McNeill's volume was published in 1953 under the auspices of the Royal Institute of International Affairs, and the author acknowledges "the scrutiny of a number of individuals familiar with the events narrated, but who must, according to Chatham House policy, remain anonymous." It is an admirable book. Its limitation lies in its pub-

205

lishing date, which was prior to the time when the Yalta and Potsdam volumes, the Stalin correspondence, and even Churchill's last volume (*Triumph and Tragedy*) became available.

It is to Feis that I owe a number of startling discoveries, for instance that Russia, when it initially subscribed to the Atlantic Charter, did so with an important reservation (see the note on p. x); that Churchill told or reminded Roosevelt in 1942 that Russia's acceptance of the Charter had been on the basis that it would regain the enlarged territories it occupied at the time of the German attack (ch.3, n.11); and that Roosevelt recalled to Churchill after Yalta that it had been understood there that the Lublin Poles were to have preponderance over the non-Communists (ch.4, n.28). Feis acknowledged the use of State Department records and of papers in possession of Mr. Harriman that have not yet been published.

With regard to Poland, the books *The Rape of Poland—Pattern of Soviet Conquest* by former Prime Minister Mikolajczyk ch.1, n.11) and *Defeat in Victory* by former Ambassador Ciechanowski (ch.3, n.23) are invaluable, also for information that does not necessarily support the wisdom of the policies of the erstwhile Polish government-in-exile, e.g., the detailed evidence of how persuasively Churchill urged a conciliatory policy toward Russia upon the reluctant Polish leaders (ch.3, n.33, n.43). On the Katyn massacre, the House *Hearings* (ch.1, n.9) are the most useful source because they contain both the Polish and the Russian cases, in addition to material not found in either. A useful summary is also found in Zawodny's *Death in the Forest* (ch.3, n.16). There are some unexplained discrepancies between the original Polish documents, the House *Hearings*, and Zawodny's book as regards the exact composition of the prisoner population of Starobielsk, Kozielsk, and Ostashkov.

Of course, the memoirs of the participants in the various negotiations are prime source material: the Hull *Memoirs* (ch.1, n.8), Churchill's *The Second World War* (ch.3, n.5), the Truman *Memoirs* (ch.4, n.30), also Sherwood's *Roosevelt and Hopkins* (ch.2, n.1)—where many years ago I first came upon the record of the Stalin-Hopkins conversations—and, to a lesser extent, Byrnes's *Speaking Frankly* (ch.1, n.10), Stettinius's *Roosevelt and the Russians—The Yalta Conference* (see p. 193), and the *Forrestal Diaries* (ch.1, n.4), and Leahy's *I Was There* (ch.5, n.12).

Principal Sources

Although both Feis and McNeill provide admirable descriptions and analyses of the Yalta Conference, I have relied primarily on the State Department's volume *The Conferences of Malta and Yalta* (ch.1, n.1). The same is true of the Department's volumes *Conferences of Cairo and Tehran* (ch.3, n.30) and *Conference of Berlin (Potsdam) 1945* (ch.2, n.1.). Chapter 2 is, of course, entirely drawn from the Potsdam volume. In addition, I have occasionally consulted the useful *Documents on American Foreign Relations, 1944-1945* (ch.5, n.44) and the fascinating *Documents on German Foreign Policy* (ch.3, n.1), which were published by the Department of State.

The Russians have "scooped" the West with their official publication of the *Stalin Correspondence* (ch.3, n.19), which contains the texts of all the important wartime messages between Stalin on the one hand and Churchill, Attlee, Roosevelt, and Truman on the other, and thus constitutes important primary source material. I was informed that the texts are authentic. On the other hand, one message from Churchill to Stalin, which is contained in *Triumph and Tragedy* (ch.3, n.5), is not found in the *Stalin Correspondence*, apparently because it was sent after the end of the war in Europe.

For many years I had collected clippings from the *New York Times* on materials related to the beginnings of the Cold War. For this study, I also methodically went through the Department's microfilmed files of the *New York Times* for the period between Yalta and Potsdam, and for part of that period also consulted the records of official radio broadcasts of Russia and Germany. It was while doing this that I came upon the historical oddity of Göbbels's authorship of the term "iron curtain" in February 1945 (ch.4, n.20). On the subject of military operations, I have relied on Wilmot's *The Struggle for Europe* (ch.3, n.48). In the matter of the surrender negotiations in Switzerland, Wilmot's shorter account contains some facts not mentioned by Feis, so I have gone back to the primary source adduced by Wilmot, since Feis's sources are not stated (ch.4, n.24).

On the history of the San Francisco Conference, I have used Ruth Russell's *A History of the United Nations Charter* (ch.4, n.5), also for corroboration of the information on Argentina obtained from the survey volumes. In the same manner I have used, for reference purposes, *The Realignment of Europe* (ch.5, n.62), a companion volume to the excellent one by McNeill, also published under the

207

auspices of the Royal Institute of International Affairs, and also edited by Arnold Toynbee, but of more uneven quality. *Tito* by Vladimir Dedijer (ch.5, n.28), and the angry exchange between the Yugoslav and Soviet Communist Parties, reproduced in *The Soviet-Yugoslav Dispute* (ch.5, n.58), issued by the Royal Institute, were the sources from which my inferences were drawn regarding Stalin's apparent willingness to carve up the Balkans.

Source materials on the history of Russia's request for a $6 billion credit are limited. The *Yalta Papers* (ch.1, n.1) contain some revealing documents on the earliest reactions in the United States government, but more will become available when the 1945 volume of *Foreign Relations of the United States* is published. I have used the President's reports on Lend-Lease as primary sources, but have had to rely on Deane's rather chatty *Strange Alliance* (ch.6, n.10) for some facts that cannot yet be documented. One of the most revealing bits of information came to my attention when General Smith's *My Three Years in Moscow* (ch.6, n.38) was first serialized in the *New York Times,* and his account of a conversation in 1947 disclosed that it had taken us over a year to respond to the January 1945 request. (It appears, however, that Stalin's statement that the request had not even been acknowledged is in error. On this point, we must await more published documentation—also on how it could happen that a renewed Russian request could get "lost" in the United States bureaucracy.) The Senate *Hearings* (ch.6, n.33) and Mosely's excellent essays on the frustrations of United States postwar planners (ch.5, n.77; ch.6, n.32) round out the principal sources of this chapter.

It will not have escaped the reader that I have refrained from making judgments in the narrative, except when it is a matter of evaluating the evidence itself, as in the case of the meaning and wording of the "ambiguous compromise" at Yalta on the formation of a Polish Provisional Government of National Unity. There are, however, some exceedingly interesting judgments of the events contained in Feis and McNeill, and I have placed these in the notes whenever they seemed particularly relevant. For instance, both of these professional historians seem to agree in their evaluation of the Declaration on Liberated Europe as a clear case of misunderstanding, and I have

208

quoted extensively from them in note 18 to Chapter 4 because these comments seem important. Similarly, I have picked up in note 19 extensive quotes from Captain Thorneycroft's speech about the Polish settlement because it seems to contain useful insights that deserve consideration. I owe this quotation to Norman Graebner's interesting documentary study, *Cold War Diplomacy* (ch.4, n.19). Also, McNeill's comment on the importance of Italy as a precedent for the occupation policies in the Balkans (ch.5, n.9) makes explicit a judgment that is perhaps implicitly contained in the historical facts as they have been presented.

Index